THE BOOK OF
INCENSE

THE BOOK OF INCENSE

Enjoying the Traditional Art of Japanese Scents

KIYOKO MORITA

KODANSHA INTERNATIONAL
Tokyo • New York • London

Photographs are reproduced with permission from Shoyeido Incense Company, Tokyo Kokuritsu Hakubutsukan, Tokyo Gendai Bijutsukan, Tokugawa Bijutsukan, Shoso-in, and Tankosha.

Quotations on pp. 37, 38, and 54 are from *The Tale of Genji* translated by Edward Seidensticker, published by Knopf; copyright © 1978. The Genji-koh chapter titles appearing from p. 92 are taken from *Genji Days*, by Edward Seidensticker, published by Kodansha International; copyright © 1977.
The second quotation on p. 38 is from *The Pillow Book of Sei Shonagon* translated by Ivan Morris, published by Penguin Books; copyright © 1970.

Distributed in the United States by Kodansha America, Inc., 575 Lexington Avenue, New York, N.Y. 10022, and in the United Kingdom and continental Europe by Kodansha Europe Ltd., 95 Aldwych, London WC2B 4JF. Published by Kodansha International Ltd., 17-14 Otowa 1-chome, Bunkyo-ku, Tokyo 112-8652, and Kodansha America, Inc.

ISBN 4-7700-2389-8

To my mother and father,
my siblings, and all of my dear friends
on both sides of the Pacific.

Acknowledgements

This book would not have been possible were it not for the help of a number of friends and colleagues. I would like to thank Masataka Hata and members of Shoyeido Incense company for their advice and support. Master Sogen Hachiya and members of the Kyoto Shinobu-kai have kindly shared their knowledge of incense with many students of incense in both Japan and America. Members of the Boston Incense Study Group have been a constant source of enthusiasm and encouragement. I was very fortunate to have Meagan Calogeras of Kodansha International as my editor. Meagan has spent many long hours revising often incomprehensible drafts of this book, and I thank her for her patience and insightful suggestions. I would also like to thank my friend Mike Caine for correcting my English (no small feat for an engineer), and for generating a number of the illustrations.

CONTENTS

Foreword

Satsuki matsu
Hanatachibana no
Ka o kageba
Mukashi no hito no
Sode no ka zo suru

  Fragrance of the orange
Flowering at last in June
  Wafts through the summer night
The memory of scented sleeves
Of someone long ago.

    Kokinshu III:139 Anonymous

   The fragrance of remembered scenes draws us power-fully. Taste, touch, smell—these are the most primordial of our senses, the ones that reach back beyond the rational to move us in inexplicable ways. The most evanescent of them, smell, has been refined by certain civilizations—the French, for instance, and the Japanese—into olfactory art, an investigation of essences, a pride in expertise. Kiyoko Morita's book is about the Japanese and their cult of "listening to incense." She explains the history and practice of incense appreciation and then goes on to detail the ingredients and rules of an art/game that is perhaps more recherché than any other. Her book is fun to read, as bright and light as a whiff of pure plum blossom, not insistent like *hyakubu*, the famous "hundred-pace" incense of ancient Japan. The game of incense guessing is also fun to play, as I learned some years ago thanks to Ms. Morita's kind invitation. As in all matters of cultural appreciation, one needs to enter into the spirit of the thing. The fragrances of smoldering aromatic woods, each subtly different, make it easy to do just that.

Physical and social enjoyment, refinement of the senses, contact with an exotic cult—these are clearly among the attractions of Kodo, the Way of Incense. But under them lies the deeper attraction associated with fragrance itself, whether of the lilacs in the dooryard or the offertory incense stick burning before the altar. Fragrances remind us of home—the garden, the embrace of scented sleeves, the memory of one who has passed away—and in this resides their true power.

Edwin A. Cranston
Harvard University

Introduction

Of the five physical human senses, the majority of us probably least appreciate the sense of smell. Although we may wrinkle our nose at a disagreeable smell, the very existence of such odors plays an important role in our lives. Sometimes they can be warning signals in situations, such as darkness, where our other senses are not effective. Not only does the sense of smell have a practical function, but the absence of smell would certainly make our lives much less interesting.

We are often not aware that we pursue certain fragrances out of unconscious preferences. We may be drawn to the aroma of fresh coffee brewing, even though we may be tea drinkers, or to the fresh smell coming from an open window overlooking greenery when we have been cooped up in a closed room. We may prefer floral or citrus scents to the smell of bacon and eggs to rouse ourselves from sleep first thing in the morning. The sense of smell is also strongly linked to memory; for just as visual images trigger remembrance of one's past experiences, so too do smells. Whatever our preferences, our interpretations of smells are subjective, dependent on our genetic makeup, personality, and experiences.

From ancient times, many kinds of smells and fragrances have permeated human life, and people have discriminated among a variety of them. Yet, ironically, the more civilization developed, the narrower the range of smells grew to be, until the creation of artificially odorless environments became the norm. At certain points in history, people devoted much energy and spent considerable amounts of money in the pursuit and creation of new scents and fragrances to replace the old smells. Their efforts resulted in perfumes in the West and incense in the Orient.

While we now perceive expensive perfumes as essential elements of the world of fashion and romance, perfume was originally created to cover body odors at a time when modern ideas of hygiene were unknown, access to bathing was not readily available, and bathing itself was actually considered harmful. In Asia, incense was also used to camouflage unwelcome smells, but more frequently it was associated with religious functions. Real perfume, because of its costliness, still remains largely in the realm of well-heeled society, but incense, on the other hand, has become a part of popular culture.

In Japan, an art form grew up around the use of incense, and only in Japan is incense used to enhance the appreciation of the four seasons. Unlike perfume, the fragrance of incense can be quite faint and subtle; so much so, in fact, that we can understand why the Chinese used the expression "listening to incense" (*wenxiang*) rather than "smelling incense." This term was adopted by the ancient Japanese incense connoisseurs, so that in Japanese today, one also "listens to incense" (*mon-koh*, the Japanese pronunciation of the Chinese expression, wenxiang). We will use the expression "listening to incense" throughout this book.

Because the varieties and uses of incense in Japan are unique, we will refer to Japanese incense as *koh*, and the ceremonial appreciation of koh as *Koh-do* (Incense Ceremony). Many other Japanese art forms—tea ceremony, flower arrangement, and Kabuki, for example—are relatively well known outside Japan. The incense ceremony, on the other hand, still remains much of a mystery. Koh-do allows you to open up to new realms of the sense of smell—a world fragrant with psychological benefits. If you can suspend any preconceptions about incense to fully experience the ceremony of koh, the happy result will be the ability to appreciate "incense time" as you would "tea time" for relaxation, refreshment, and communion with others.

Umegae (Plum Branch), by Mitsunori Tosa, early Edo period (17th century). An illustration from Chapter 32 of *The Tale of Genji*. Prince Genji prepares for an incense contest, blending incense himself, to celebrate the entry of his daughter by Lady Akashi into service at the court. He is shown here discussing details before the game with another courtier who will be the judge. The Tokugawa Art Museum, Aichi Prefecture.

The most famous named *jinkoh* (*meikoh*) of all, enjoyed by shoguns and nobility: Ranjatai. Designated "Treasure" from the Shoso-in, Nara.

MAIN INGREDIENTS OF KOH

1. *Haisokoh* The thin, hairlike root of *haiso*, a plant native to southern China. **2. Sandalwood** This fragrant, yellowish wood, which comes from a type of Asian evergreen tree, has insect-repelling properties. **3. *Kyara*** The most highly valued of the six kinds of *jinkoh* (aloeswood). **4. *Jinkoh (jin/aloeswood)*** The soft resinous wood of an East Indian evergreen tree, also known as agalloch, agalwood, and other names, which has been buried in the ground and transformed by a natural aging process. **5. *Kara-mokkoh*** Roots of a herbaceous plant resembling thistles, found mostly in temperate and cooler regions of Eurasia. **6. Cassia and Cinnamon** The dried barks taken from young shoots of two types of trees in the laurel family. Cassia, in particular, is one of the oldest known spices. Native to Assam and northern Burma, it was in use by the Chinese as early as 2700 B.C., and is sometimes known as Chinese cinnamon. **7. Conch shells** Used chiefly as a preservative, the shells are ground and added to other ingredients in making blended-incense balls. **8. Musk** A strong-smelling substance obtained from the abdominal sac of a type of East Asian deer. *This ingredient is no longer used in modern incense.* **9. Myrrh** An aromatic bitter gum resin obtained from certain plants found in Africa and Arabia, myrrh has been used since ancient times as an ingredient in incense and perfume, as well

as for medicinal purposes. **10. Star anise** Native to southern China and Vietnam, star anise is the dried fruit of an evergreen tree belonging to the magnolia family. It is not unlike anise and fennel in smell and taste, and is used in Asian cuisine. **11. Benzoin** A balsamic resin derived from various trees belonging to the Styrax family, growing primarily in the tropical forests of Sumatra, Java, and Thailand. **12. Patchouli** An East Indian shrubby mint that yields a fragrant essential oil. **13. *Rei–ryokoh*** The dried stems and leaves of a kind of mint plant common to central Asia. **14. Cloves** The dried flower buds of a tropical tree indigenous to the Moluccas of Indonesia, but now widely cultivated. **15. Frankincense** A gum resin containing volatile oil, obtained from trees growing chiefly in northeastern Africa and southern Arabia, valued by the ancients for its fumigating and embalming properties, as well as as an incense ingredient. **16. *Kansho*** A rhizome of an East Indian aromatic plant. **17. Borneo Camphor** A resinous crystalline substance derived from the camphor tree.

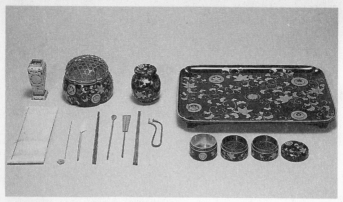

Gold lacquer incense tray and utensils.

Gold lacquer rack for scenting kimono.

Gold lacquer box with spring mountain design for storing wrapped incense wood pieces.

Gold lacquer incense "pillow." The box, containing a censer, was placed near a pillow so that hair could be placed over it and scented during sleep.

Far right: lacquer censer with silver mesh chimney used originally for burning incense for pleasure (*soradaki*) and for scenting clothes. It is now used in *Koh-do* to bring heated charcoal to the incense ceremony room before transferring charcoal pieces to smaller censers.

Left and middle: ceramic censers with designs of emblems from the game *Genji-koh*.

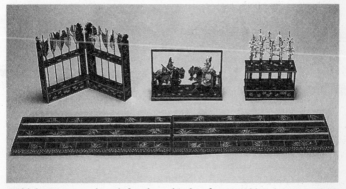

Gold lacquer gameboard for three kinds of competitive incense games (*kumikoh*): horse racing, archery, and "noteworthy places."

THE MAKING OF INCENSE PRODUCTS

Fine-Cut Incense Wood

Top: Chopping *jinkoh*.
Bottom: Sifting chopped *jinkoh* through a sieve for use in producing other incense products.

Chipped Incense Wood

Chipping *jinkoh* (*kyara*) pieces with a special hammer and chisel. (After this step, pieces are cut still more finely.)

Joss-Stick Incense

Top: Guiding freshly-formed blended incense "sticks" onto a drying tray.
Bottom: Cutting with a bamboo spatula to a uniform size in preparation for drying.

Blended-Incense Balls

Mashing an incense blend that has already gone through the aging process.

Blended incense is rolled out onto a shallow tray and then cut into small squares.

Squares are lifted from the tray with a spatula and rounded by hand into balls.

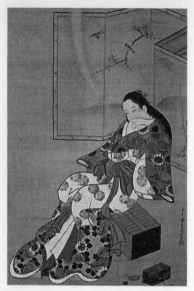

Yujo mon-koh-zu (Portrait of a Courtesan Listening to Incense), by Choshun Miyagawa, Edo period, late 18th century. Tokyo National Museum. On the floor beside the courtesan's sitting box is a *koh-bako* and incense ceremony paraphernalia. At her feet is a censer, the smoky fragrance of which can be seen rising around her bosom.

Mon-koh (Listening to Incense), by Shinsui Ito, 1950. National Museum of Modern Art, Tokyo.

I

Incense and Other Aromatic Substances

It would be no exaggeration to say that incense has existed since the beginning of human history. In the Bible, there is a reference to the "burnt offerings" that Noah made to God after the Flood, and "the Lord smelled the sweet savour" (Genesis VIII, 12:21). This aroma soothed God's anger, and for man's sake, he vowed not to curse the ground. Just imagine—there is Noah, alone with his family, one of the few selected by God to be saved from destruction. He builds an altar and burns incense—and it is this incense that keeps God from destroying mankind again! As we can see, incense played an important role from the very first in the annals of human history.

In terms of aromatics, we are probably most familiar with perfumes—*parfum* in French. Although we rarely think about heating or burning in association with perfume, it is interesting to note that the etymon of *parfum* is the Latin *perfumum*, meaning "by smoke," that is, the smoke from trees and plants. This is not strange when we realize that aromatics were important from ancient times for use in sacred rituals where they were heated to release their fragrance. Those who conducted such rituals had to purify their bodies and souls by exposing their garments to the smoke emitted by aromatics, and sometimes by rubbing aromatic ointment on themselves beforehand.

The story of the Three Kings from the Orient who brought gifts to the Christ Child is a familiar one. Two of the gifts were aromatics: frankincense and myrrh. The aromatics used in the days of both the Old and New Testament were solidified tree saps. Frankincense has a milky color and a sumptuous sweet aroma, and myrrh is dark red, pungently bitter and sweet. But their aromas are emitted only when they are heated or burnt.

In ancient Egypt, myrrh in particular among many aromatics was used in the preparation of mummies; in fact, some etymologists trace the word "mummy" back to "myrrh." Besides its practical function in embalming and sterilizing corpses, it also had religious significance, for fragrance was believed to be a messenger by which the living reached out to the souls of the dead in the nether world. It is no surprise, then, that incense should have been used for funeral rites. Sandalwood was burnt in the cremation of the Buddha, and when Christ died, a blend of aloeswood incense and myrrh was prepared. (A blend of several aromatic substances was often used for funeral rites, producing a stronger fragrance than the burning of a single substance.)

What was this myrrh, for example, that the ancient Egyptians so eagerly sought? Where did they find it? As with frankincense, people cherished myrrh for its distinctive aroma. The substance which emitted the aroma when heated was the milk and sap taken from evergreen trees, and these trees as well as those which produce storax and benzoin (both aromatic resins) all grew in Arabia. Other aromatic woods were produced only in India, China, and Southeast Asia. As aromatics became an important part of people's lives, considerable wealth was spent and goods bartered in pursuit of them, and the aromatic-wood supplying regions prospered from trading in this new commodity with ancient Egypt, Greece, and Rome, where such trees did not grow.

The use of aromatics for pleasure in ancient Egypt, Greece, Rome, and the Orient played a great part in commerce and cultural exchange. Among many historical figures who enthusiastically sought heady fragrances was the Roman emperor Nero. He is said to have installed wall fixtures in his palatial quarters to entertain his guests with a shower of fragrant oil or flower petals. Some rooms were carpeted with flower petals. His wife, also fond of using perfumed lotion, had a personal consultant who was responsible for finding the most extravagant aromatics. The Macedonian king Alexander the Great was an eager collector of aromatics, and it was precisely the search for them that made him push further and further eastward on his famous expeditions to Greece and Persia.

There is a well-known legend that King Asoka, a benevolent king of India around 250 B.C., fell deathly ill, and only after the successful conclusion of a seven-day desperate search for the only believed cure—storax incense—was the King saved. The King's retainers were said to have rejoiced and danced with helmets made of the wood from which storax incense is formed.

We can find various accounts of the use of aromatics and incense in China too. A legendary account from 5 B.C. has it that a ruler of China was brought to ruin by his obsession with a fragrant court lady, whose body gave out a heady aroma. She became the standard of aromatic beauty. Another tale tells of a beautiful concubine named Chao Fei-yen, who would scent her body with incense to attract the attention of the Han emperor Wu in 150 B.C. Around A.D. 8, another beautiful concubine in T'ang China named Yanguifei used an extravagant amount of aloeswood to build her pavilion and to scent her body to camouflage any undesirable body odors.

For millennia, people of many cultures have felt a desire to remain eternally young, and aphrodisiacs have been sought to that end. At times, the purpose of obtaining such aphrodisiacs went beyond individual interest and became a matter of ruling families wishing to maintain their political and social control through extended blood-lines. Sought-after aphrodisiacs included musk, cloves, myrrh, and aloeswood. Some were applied to the body, some taken orally, and others were mixed in oil and burnt.

These spices and aromatics became so valuable that European merchants fought for the rights to trade in them. Such countries as Morocco and Ceylon, which produced abundant quantities of cloves and cinnamon, prospered, but they were also exploited. Japan possessed little valued spices and incense wood, so instead she was destined to remain an importer and consumer, enjoying items for religious and artistic purposes.

II

Japan's Encounter with Incense

INCENSE AND BUDDHISM

While the aesthetic practice of Koh-do (literally, the Way of Incense, and commonly translated as Incense Ceremony) is a product of Japanese culture, the incense ingredients used for Koh-do are not indigenous to Japan. Unlike tea, which was originally imported from China but was later cultivated in Japan, incense wood still comes from the tropics of Southeast Asia. The oldest record of incense appreciation in Japan appears in A.D. 595 in the first Japanese chronicle *Nihonshoki* (Chronicles of Japan): "Ligh-aloes wood [aloeswood] drifted ashore on the island of Awaji. It was six feet in circumference. The people of the island, being unacquainted with aloeswood, used it with other firewood to burn for cooking; the smoky vapor spread its perfume far and wide. In wonderment, they presented it to the Empress."

This aromatic aloeswood is called *jinkoh* in Japanese, or sometimes simply *jin*, meaning "sinking-in-water" incense. (*Jinkoh* comes from a Sanskrit word meaning "heavy.") Not all wood the Japanese refer to as jinkoh sinks in the water, however. If it is not oily or resinous enough it may float, and be less aromatic and thus of less value.) What gives jinkoh such an aromatic property? No one really knows. It was once believed that it formed only over a long period of time after an old and diseased aloeswood tree had died, fallen, and been buried under leaves and soil. However, more recently this aromatic property has been discovered in living trees belonging to the daphne family. The color of jinkoh is generally dark brown or black. The more resinous the wood, the darker, heavier, and more aromatic it becomes. This biochemical change is extremely rare, however, and it takes a highly experienced person to find such aromatic wood either buried underground, or in a living tree in the jungle.

When the islanders of Awaji (near Kobe) took the "Ligh-aloes wood" to the court because of the remarkably fragrant aroma of its smoke, Prince Shotoku (A.D. 574–622) immediately recognized it as jin, the precious incense wood. Incense use had been introduced to Japan along with Buddhism by the middle of the sixth century via the Korean peninsula and was already a part of the higher classes. As a zealous supporter of Buddhism, Prince Shotoku was well acquainted with this fragrance from Buddhist rituals, which could not be performed without incense.

During the Nara period (A.D. 710–794), political power fell into the hands of the leaders who supported Buddhism. Buddhist rituals came to be incorporated into state ceremonies and imperial court functions, which had been based on traditional rites of Shinto, the indigenous religion of Japan. Incense was now burnt both as an offering to the Buddha and in order to purify the ritual site. Only after the Meiji Restoration (1868), when the reins of government were restored to the emperor from a feudal clan, was the tradition of offering incense during imperial functions abandoned. Thus, the Meiji Restoration, with its emphasis on things Western, ironically marks the return of incense offering to its original use as part of Buddhist rituals. Unfortunately, this also gave rise to a popular association of the smell of incense with death—with funerals and graveyards—which to some extent still holds today.

The incense used in ancient Japanese Buddhist rituals was at first a mixture of five to seven chipped aromatic materials, such as jinkoh, sandalwood, cloves, cinnamon, and camphor. (See *Shokoh*, page 59.) The amount and combination of these materials varied slightly depending on the Buddhist sect. This kind of incense was sprinkled directly on hot ash containing burning charcoal. After the technique of making joss-stick incense was introduced to Japan in the sixteenth century (some say by Koreans, others by Chinese), it became as common as chipped incense in Buddhist rituals for the ease with which it was burned. Although joss-stick incense was also burned for pleasure, the Japanese have long associated it with Buddhist rituals. Fragrance was believed to help invoke the Buddha's presence and summon forth his peaceful world.

Two large pieces of jinkoh are still preserved in an eighth-century imperial storehouse on the grounds of Todaiji temple in Nara. The larger piece was a gift to the temple from Empress Komyo in A.D. 756 and is named Todaiji, although it is popularly called Ranjatai. Originally weighing about 13 kilograms, it now weighs 11.6 kilograms because small pieces were cut off from time to time by the emperors and shoguns for their own use and to reward loyal retainers. Among the fortunate recipients were said to be the shogun Ashikaga Yoshimasa (1436-90; see "The Warriors' Way: The Birth of Koh-do," page 40) and Oda Nobunaga (1534-82), and the emperor Meiji (1852-1912). Tags on Ranjatai mark the places where the pieces were cut off for the three. The rumor that Oda Nobunaga sent a troop of his emissaries to the priests of

Todaiji temple to negotiate a piece for his personal use has made Ranjatai an especially interesting item for visitors. If we were to burn a piece from this wood today, we would be able to smell the unadulterated, exquisite aroma of this jinkoh just as the shoguns had smelled it centuries ago. This is not possible with perfume, which oxidizes and loses its fragrance after about twenty-five years. The large pieces of incense wood and incense burners stored along with many other exquisite items imported from Asia and the Far East are clear indications that incense was sought after and valued during the feudal era of Japanese history.

THE COURTIERS' WAY

Largely as a result of interest in Buddhism, political and cultural intercourse between China's T'ang Dynasty and Japan flourished during the Nara and early Heian period (794–1192) until Japan stopped sending official envoys to China. Throughout this time, Chinese influence on the lives of the Japanese aristocracy was profound. Japan continued to assimilate Buddhism, retaining the use of incense in the ceremonies. One early exponent of ceremonial incense use was the Chinese priest Ganjin (A.D. 688–763), who had been invited to set up Buddhist doctrines for the Japanese. Numerous attempts to cross the Japan Sea had cost him his eyesight, but on his fourth attempt he finally succeeded in reaching the Japanese islands. Along with the Buddhist creed, he introduced various uses of spices, as well as blended incense and its recipes, which was already popular in China. The Chinese had been using blended incense for pleasure and medicinal purposes apart from religion for some time, and the Heian courtiers quickly adopted the recipes. It was exciting to experience China—the most exotic place in the world at the time— by re-creating Chinese fragrances.

This new way of using fragrance apart from of religious functions was called *soradaki* (empty burning), differentiating it from *sonae-koh* (incense offering to Buddha). The emptiness refers, of course, to the lack of a religious pur-

Incense burner, bronze with lotus design, Kamakura period (12th century). Ryuko-in Temple, Koyasan. This type of incense burner was used by priests in Buddhist rituals.

pose. The appreciation of incense, for example by scenting a room or a garment, or by playing incense-comparison games, developed into the art of incense, or Koh-do. Some of these games and practices of Koh-do are reserved for another chapter.

The world's first novel, *The Tale of Genji*, which was written by Lady Murasaki Shikibu in eleventh-century Japan, provides us with valuable insight into how incense was appreciated during the Heian period, when it was at the height of its use for pleasure. In one scene Prince Genji, the main character of the novel, seeking a cure for malaria, pays a visit to a temple in the northern hills of Kyoto. The bishop at the temple there burns incense as a sign of welcome for his guest. Prince Genji notices both the soradaki and sonae-koh and muses, "An enchanting fragrance drifted through the air, mixing the exquisite aroma of incense from the altar." A religious man had prepared fragrance as hospitality, in addition to the burning of incense at the altar.

Soradaki refers not only to incense that is heated for enjoyment but also to the scenting of garments. Judging from the many references to scented clothes that we find both in poetry and prose writings of the Heian period, we know that the scenting of robes was a common practice among the courtiers. This kind of scenting was done with a large censer and incense in the form of balls, and required almost an entire night. The censer was placed in a basin filled with water primarily to prevent fires. However, the dampness also helped the fragrance adhere to the cloth. The basin was lidded with a metal net covered by a large basket made of bamboo or silver. The robes to be scented were draped over the basket. If the robes were not scented satisfactorily, they could be partially rescented by using a smaller censer, as described in another part of *The Tale of Genji*: ". . . once more with a miniature brazier that he held for a moment inside each sleeve . . ." In her essay, *The Pillow Book*, written about 1002, Lady Shonagon observed, "To wash one's hair, make one's toilet, and put on scented robes; even if not a soul sees one, these preparations still produce an inner pleasure." Clearly, garment scenting was done for personal pleasure.

Through experimentation, the courtiers began to adapt the use of incense in still more innovative ways. Besides using it for cosmetic and medicinal purposes, they burned incense to enhance the enjoyment of the season, or to heighten an occasion or the mood of a gathering. Poems from *Kokinshu*, the first Japanese imperial anthology of poems (ca. A.D. 905), illustrate the courtiers' enchantment with scents.

In the moonlight
Where are the plum blossoms?
Let their fragrance guide you.

The fragrance—
more alluring than the color—
Whose scented sleeves have brushed
the blossoms in my garden?

We can see how the Heian courtiers admired the fragrance of the plum blossoms as much—if not more—than the color, and how in addition to auditory and visual conventions, they also used the sense of smell. A scented evening breeze or a whiff of a fragrant kimono sleeve was enough to begin composing. To the Heian courtiers, the notion of beauty incorporated the sense of smell along with visual aesthetics. Such an awareness of fragrance meant that scents were an essential element in their lives.

In time, the Heian aristocrats were thrilled to discover that the original incense recipes brought to Japan by the priest Ganjin could be modified to create their own delicate fragrances. It was like adapting a dessert recipe to include one's favorite ingredients. By blending their own combination of ingredients, they were able to fine-tune their appreciation of scents, and they joined in contests to compare their creations with one another. Through these contests and other games, they were able to enjoy incense more fully. This was the beginning of appreciating incense for its fragrance and the spiritual communion offered in its preparation.

THE WARRIORS' WAY: THE BIRTH OF KOH-DO

The end of the Kamakura period (1185-1333) marks another significant shift in the history of incense in Japan. The term "incense" had come to mean blended incense (*nerikoh* in Japanese), but now people reverted to the burning of incense wood itself. This aromatic wood was the jinkoh ("sink-in-water" incense) mentioned earlier. It was during the subsequent Muromachi period (1336-1573) that enjoying the fragrance of a heated piece of incense wood according to set rules and principles became known in Japan as "listening" to incense.

This set the stage for the establishment of Koh-do, which begins with shogun Ashikaga Yoshimasa, a great patron of such arts as the tea ceremony, flower arrangement, and Noh drama, who asked his trusted vassal and chief military advisor Shino Soshin to evaluate and classify all of the incense that they used. Soshin organized and set up rules for this form of aesthetic practice with the help and advice of Sanjonishi Sanetaka, an eminent scholar, poet, and minister under the shogun who was also in charge of all matters relating to incense at the imperial court. Together they classified the pieces as "Ashikaga Shogun's Collection of 120," "Incense Selected by Emperors," "Shino Family Collection," and the like. They also developed games and rules for incense-appreciation parties.

The social elite of the time—warriors and male aristocrats—often conducted incense-appreciation parties during which they were able to hone their aesthetic senses. (Some warlords, however, rapaciously collected the precious wood to show off their wealth, an indication of the great value that society placed on the possession of incense.)

Around the fifteenth century, the Japanese connoisseurs of koh began to use the term "listen to incense." Why this phrase instead of "smelling incense"? Japanese themselves have often asked this question. One scholar of the Edo period (1603-1868) wrote in response to a layperson's question:

"'Listening to incense' had its origin in the Chinese language, and one did not find such an expression in the Japanese language. The word 'smell' was considered a traditional and fine word. One 'smells' fragrances of things and 'smells'

blended incense, too. For instance, poems in Kokinshu *refer to 'smelling' the fragrance of flowering citrus-orange blossoms. Also, in the chapter entitled 'Umegae' [Plum Branch] in* The Tale of Genji, *it is written: 'to smell the depth of incense mixed by various people.' We cannot find such an expression as 'listen' in our old texts. People today, without having proper knowledge, seem to take it for granted that to 'smell' fragrance is a vulgar word, but this is wrong. They mis-understand it. To say 'listen to incense' is just a popular and fashionable thing to do now, but it is not a truly refined phrase at all."*

This scholar argued that the Chinese phrase wenxiang, listening to incense, was a word imported from China. Since he was a Japanese language specialist, he most likely considered the use of the imported word somewhat vulgar or simply faddish. If he had traced the original source of the phrase "listening to incense," this scholar would have understood the reasoning behind the connoisseurs' choice of the phrase, and indeed they had made a rational choice and had not merely been following a fad.

In fact, the idea of listening to incense may be traced even further back to a section of the fourteen-volume Mahayana sutra of Buddhism. There, in a dialogue between the bodhisattva Monju (a Buddhist saint of wisdom and intellect) and Yuima-kitsu (a wealthy Indian Buddhist layman, also known for his wisdom and intellect), Yuima learns that in the Buddha's world everything is fragrant like incense, including the words of Buddha. *Fragrance* and *incense* are synonymous, and Buddha's words of teaching are incense. Therefore, bodhisattvas listen to Buddha's words, in the form of incense, instead of smelling them. When incense use for Buddhism was introduced to China, Chinese people apparently adopted this expression: incense is something one listens to, rather than smells.

In Japan, as incense wood became more popular than blended incense, the Japanese retained the literal meaning of the characters *wen xiang* 聞香, but changed the grammatical order so that the phrase in Japanese became *koh o kiku* or *mon-koh* (listen to incense). Whatever its historical roots, considering how precious and exotic this incense wood must have been in fourteenth-century Japan, we can imagine how "listen" must have had a more appealing sound to the warrior and male aristocrat classes in expressing their practice of Koh-do.

THE ESTABLISHMENT OF INCENSE SCHOOLS: AN ART FORM FOR ALL

By the end of the Muromachi period, Koh-do had established itself as an organized art form, different from the informal appreciation of incense during Heian times. It wasn't until the middle of the Edo period (1603-1867) that Koh-do reached its peak of popularity. Incense appreciation flourished in the capital city of Edo under the Tokugawa regime. This was no coincidence, as the traditional courtly arts patronized by the Ashikaga shoguns in the fifteenth century—Noh drama, the tea ceremony, poetry, and flower arrangement, as well as incense appreciation—were now practiced by the Tokugawa elite (the shogunal court, the regional lords or daimyo, and their samurai retainers), and by the newly emerging urban merchant class. Koh-do, which was previously dominated by males, also became popular among elite women, such as the shogun's daughters, and in some cases by commoners, including courtesans. Incense appreciation came to be considered a "suitable feminine pleasure," along with playing the *koto* (Japanese lyre) and performing the tea ceremony. In fact, it was recommended as the very first art form an accomplished courtesan should master, followed by tea ceremony, poetry, and the playing of musical instruments.

An abundance of references to the use of incense can be found in the literature of this period. And in the woodblock prints of the "floating world" (an epithet for the social flux and decadence of the time), or *ukiyoe*, we find courtesans as well as the townsmen of Edo portrayed using incense. It was fashionable among men pretending to elegance to carry incense in their kimono sleeves as a way of attracting women. They used good incense, for example, *kyara*, meaning "jin of the highest quality," to perfume their robes. In the city of Edo, *kyara* became a highly complimentary word: kyara woman meant beautiful woman; kyara clogs meant high-quality clogs, and so forth. Stories circulated about those who visited the pleasure quarters and exchanged incense with courtesans after spending an evening with them, or even of lost lovers being reunited by identifying each other's scent.

Among the art objects of the Edo period found in museums today are many incense burners, incense containers, and exquisite lacquered incense boxes; further evidence for the flourishing popularity of Koh-do. Parents often prepared such a box containing all of the necessary utensils and paraphernalia for their daughter when she was to be married. Incense pillows and sachets also came into common use during this period.

With its increasing popularity among the common people, incense appreciation came to be governed by an elaborate set of rules and manners taught by professional masters and described in specialized books. Incense connoisseurs who engaged professionally in the instruction of

Koh-do justified the legitimacy of their teachings by establishing schools headed by masters, who in turn made special claims to their own expertise. Participation in Koh-do was thus organized into a pyramidal system. The legitimation of these schools was derived (perhaps fictitiously) from the two early founders of Koh-do: Shino Soshin and Sanjonishi Sanetaka, who probably had had no idea that they would be put at the top of such a school system. In the Edo period, these two founders represented the two schools of Koh-do: the Shino School (Shino Soshin), representing a warrior style with its emphasis on rigorous rules and spiritual training, and the Oie School (Sanjonishi Sanetaka), featuring courtly games derived from a more poetical spirit. These subordinate branches, too, carefully trained a corps of students in the traditional techniques and skills of appreciating and identifying incense. As is common in the traditional arts of Japan, the teachings of Koh-do were very closely guarded and were transmitted orally from the masters to the disciples only when the latter reached a certain level of proficiency. This hierarchical system still prevails today in the traditional arts.

The masters who headed these schools during the Edo period wrote "textbooks" about Koh-do, but because of the secretive nature of the teachings, such books outlined only the superficial aspects of the ceremony, such as the deportment required of participants, the sequence of steps during the ceremony, and the necessary utensils and objects. Little was explained about the characteristics of various scents. Nor were the spiritual and philosophical aspects, also an important part of incense appreciation in Koh-do, taught with any clarity. Over time, these qualities lost their importance. Through these games of identifying fragrances, people focused primarily on enhancing their incense-identification abilities and acquiring exquisitely crafted incense paraphernalia. Many of the incense games that are played today were created during this period. (You'll get a chance to try out some games later.)

THE DECLINE AND REVIVAL OF KOH-DO

Koh-do began its decline in popularity after the middle of the nineteenth century. The disintegration of the Tokugawa shogunate's hegemony, the crumbling of feudal society, the reopening of the country to the West, and the ensuing Westernization all contributed to the eclipse of the traditional arts. Particularly Koh-do, in the process of reaching the masses, had become too commercialized, with incense games emphasizing technical skill or ritualistic elements over development of aesthetic appreciation. In addition, the scarcity of high-quality ingredients necessary to produce incense probably contributed to its demise—a fate not suffered by the tea ceremony and flower arrangement arts.

After the Meiji Restoration, most incense masters could no longer earn a living by teaching Koh-do and turned to other means of supporting themselves. Incense ceremonies remained unpopular until about 1920, when several descendants of the Koh-do masters began to hold incense parties in an attempt to revive the long-neglected traditions of the art. Some of them performed ceremonies at temples, where they offered incense, and others held ceremonies at the imperial household.

Then, in the early 1960s, Koh-do masters of both the Shino and Oie schools began offering classes in which people could once again learn the art of Koh. Their disciples wrote handbooks that reinterpreted the incense-appreciation games in a simpler, less intimidating style so that young people could also participate in and enjoy them. Incense shops in Kyoto, Tokyo, Osaka, and Sapporo introduced new creations of incense and modernized utensils, and they offered space for the Koh-do masters to teach classes. Many exhibitions of incense and Koh-do utensils are still sponsored by these stores. The Shoyeido incense shop in Kyoto, for example, has put on annual ceremonies, representing both the Shino and Oie schools, in large Buddhist temples since the early 1970s.

Large associations of incense groups, each publishing its own journal, have sprung up in recent years. In the fall of 1982, masters and students of Koh-do came to the United States for the first time to introduce the incense ceremony to Americans. These demonstrations were held in New York, Los Angeles, and San Francisco. Since then, numerous ceremonies have been performed in such places as Seattle, Boston, Boulder, Denver, Paris, and Frankfurt; Boston even has a small incense study group. People in other areas are also becoming interested in hosting such incense appreciation events, hinting at positive developments for the future of Koh-do.

As we see a revival of Koh-do in Japan, and its small, tentative steps abroad, and a universal interest in healthful ways to relaxation and refreshment, the timing seems right for disseminating knowledge and bringing new life to this little known art form—The Way of Appreciating High-quality Incense.

III

Varieties of
Japanese Incense

The Japanese people have been using jinkoh and jinkoh-based products, what we call koh, for centuries. Most koh products are burnt to emit a fragrance, although a few need not be, such as Japanese sachets and potpourris. Obviously jinkoh is the most important ingredient for all koh, but by combining with other substances, the Japanese have created a wonderful variety of incense; their wide-ranging shapes, colors, and sizes allow us to enjoy fragrances for different uses in our lives.

INGREDIENTS OF KOH 香料

The most common and readily available koh products come shaped as sticks, cones, coils, and spheres, and are also in sachet form. The ingredients for all of these incense products are derived from plants and animals. They are all natural ingredients, never chemically treated or processed.

Among the incense derived from plants, the most widely known is jin, mentioned earlier, but other incense is derived from the fruits, berries, and dried flower buds (such as cloves) of trees and shrubs, the roots of cinnamon and some pine trees, Sumatra camphor resin and frankincense.

Although no longer in use, the most common animal ingredients were musk and ambergris. Musk is a secretion from the abdominal sac of the male musk deer, and ambergris is a stone (calculus) formed in the body of sperm whales. There are also fragrant substances that form in certain kinds of sea shells. Considering their origins, one would not imagine that these substances would be fragrant, and indeed, scientists have not been able to determine how they came to be so aromatic. Musk by itself has an offensive smell in large quantities, but was pleasing when mixed in small amounts with other ingredients.

Some of these substances are used as incense just as they are, while others are ground into powder and blended with other ingredients. Some naturally exude fragrance, while others need to be burnt, heated, applied to the body, or taken orally for the fragrance to be released.

Incense materials often have many uses. The better-known ingredients—spices—are used in cooking, while lesser-known ingredients are often found in insecticides or medicinal cures. Indeed, incense has been of benefit to humanity in many ways and in many forms.

Japanese koh comes almost entirely from foreign sources. Then what is really Japanese about koh? The presence of jinkoh (aloeswood), alone or blended with other ingredients, and the ceremony surrounding its enjoyment make it uniquely Japanese.

JINKOH 沈香

The fragrance of jinkoh varies depending on the amount of resin in it, the part of the tree the wood comes from (the roots and branches of the same tree can differ greatly in fragrance), and the particular region of Southeast Asia the tree grows or grew in. So, in a sense, one could say there are infinitely many kinds since each piece found in the jungle is unique. This makes the task of classifying incense wood daunting, to say the least. Nevertheless, various characteristics of aromatic incense wood have been analyzed over the years in an attempt to create a working classification. Somewhat arbitrarily, incense connoisseurs of sixteenth-century Japan chose an incense wood's country of origin to classify its fragrance. The result was six categories of jinkoh: *kyara*, *rakoku*, *manaka*, *manaban*, *sumotara*, and *sasora*. Except for kyara, these names were derived from the Japanese pronunciation for the name of the country: Sumotara (Sumatra), Manaban (possibly the Malabar Coast of India), Rakoku (Thailand), Sasora (unidentified, but thought to be in the western region of India), and Manaka (Malacca). Kyara, which is believed to come from Cambodia or Vietnam, means "black" in Sanskrit.

However, since the origin of a piece of wood was not always clear, the names later came to denote six distinct fragrances or characteristics of jinkoh. Although no longer representative of countries, this classification is still called *rikkoku* (six countries), and a knowledge of these basic characteristic fragrances is considered to be important and useful in identifying and appreciating jinkoh.

Finding the appropriate words to describe a fragrance is challenging. Back in the eleventh century they also struggled, as illustrated in a passage taken from *The Tale of Genji*, in which Prince Hotaru is asked to be the judge for an incense competition hosted by Prince Genji. During the contest he describes the blended incense as "extraordinarily delightful and intriguing," "bright and original," as having "great delicacy and refinement," and so forth. Eventually he runs out of words, at which point Genji comments, "Our judge is losing his subtlety."

To help solve this problem, the connoisseurs adopted five terms associated with flavor to describe the qualities of a fragrance. They are:

1. *Sweet—Resembles the smell of honey or concentrated sugar.*
2. *Sour—Resembles the smell of plums or other acidic foods.*
3. *Hot—Resembles the smell of red pepper when put in a fire.*
4. *Salty—Resembles the smell of a towel after wiping perspiration from the brow or the lingering smell of ocean water when seaweed is dried over a fire.*
5. *Bitter—Resembles the smell of bitter herbal medicine when it is mixed or boiled.*

Using these qualities as a basis, the literati and connoisseurs appointed by shogun Ashikaga Yoshimasa in sixteenth-century Japan attempted to describe the six kinds of jinkoh fragrances as follows:

1. *KYARA* 伽羅—*A gentle and dignified smell with a touch of bitterness. The fragrance is like an aristocrat in its elegance and gracefulness.*
2. *RAKOKU* 羅国—*A sharp and pungent smell similar to san-dalwood. Its smell is generally bitter, and reminds one of a warrior.*
3. *MANAKA* 真那賀—*Smells light and enticing, changing like the mood of a woman with bitter feelings.* [Obviously the connoisseurs of this day were men!] *None of the 5 qualities (tastes) are easily detectable. The fragrance is of good quality if it disappears quickly.*

4. MANABAN 真那蛮—*Mostly sweet. The presence of sticky oil on a mica piece is often a sign that the fragrance is manaban. The smell is coarse and unrefined, just like that of a peasant.*

5. SUMOTARA 寸門多羅—*Sour at the beginning and end. Sometimes easily mistaken for kyara, it has something, however, distasteful and ill-bred about it, like a servant disguised as a noble person.*

6. SASORA 佐曽羅—*Cool and sour. Good-quality sasora is mistaken for kyara, especially when it first begins to burn. Sometimes it is so light and faint that one may think the smell has disappeared. It reminds one of a monk.*

All six types were considered to be of good quality, but kyara was particularly valued and in high demand among aficionados such as Sasaki Doyo (1306–73), a general of the early Muromachi period known as a quintessential military aristocrat and lover of extravagance and luxury. Doyo is regarded as having been one of the preeminent collectors of incense. He invested as much energy in collecting famous pieces of incense as Heian courtiers had invested in blending it.

Although these metaphors used by connoisseurs of yore for evaluating and classifying jinkoh may not be particularly helpful to us today, modern Japanese koh listeners enjoy them for their historical interest and as a way of getting in touch with Japanese interpretations from antiquity.

Meikoh 名香 (Named Incense)

Since the Heian period, all notable wood-incense pieces, whether of extremely high quality or owned by a famous person, were given names (like Ranjatai). During the early Heian years, blended incense was named by its creator. Sometimes the name was derived from a word or a phrase in a poem that depicted the image of the fragrance. During the Muromachi and Azuchi-Momoyama periods (1336–1615), when mixed incense was replaced by incense wood, the pieces were named after the persons who happened to possess them, or from popular poems. For instance, the piece known as "Haru no yo" (Spring Evening) received its name from the following poem found in the *Kokinshu*:

> An ephemeral spring dream—
> The plum's color
> Is lost in the night.
> Would it also be possible
> To hide the fragrance?

Sometimes the names given to incense pieces were completely arbitrary. For example, a piece dubbed Nakagawa,

THE BOOK OF INCENSE

owned by General Sasaki Doyo, is believed to have been named by Doyo himself after the river near his residence in Kyoto. Named pieces of wood incense were called *meiko* and were considered more valuable as a result. Doyo is said to have collected over 180 pieces of incense with such names. In some cases, incense pieces were offered to emperors and empresses to be given a name, something akin to a "christening." These pieces were called *chokumeiko*.

Even though the connoisseurs identified and classified six jinkoh fragrances as a guideline, every small piece of incense wood will smell different from any other piece unless the pieces originate from a common source, that is, from a larger piece, and are burned under similar atmospheric conditions. For our purposes, however, it is sufficient to know that there is a characteristic aroma for each particular kind of jinkoh, and one can learn to appreciate these subtle distinctions, with time and practice, by listening to them.

INCENSE PRODUCTS

Following are discussions of the koh products—their particular ingredients, the processes involved in their creation, and suggestions for effortlessly incorporating them into our lives. (See photos on pages 17–24.)

Shokoh 焼香 (Chipped Mixture)

Shokoh is a mixture of chipped aromatic substances that is burnt on Buddhist altars. The mixtures are composed of five, seven, or ten ingredients. Major ingredients include jinkoh, sandalwood, cloves, ginger, and ambergris. Since many of these ingredients are expensive, poor-quality natural ingredients are often substituted in some brands of shokoh, resulting in an inferior fragrance. A pinch or two of the chipped mixture is placed directly on hot ashes and burned.

Nerikoh 練香 (Blended-Incense Balls)

When various powdered ingredients are mixed with honey (or sometimes plum meat) and then kneaded and formed into balls, the resulting blended incense is called *nerikoh*. Moisture is critical for creating a rich fragrance, therefore honey is used instead of water to prevent the mixture from drying out.

Nerikoh sometimes contains over twenty ingredients. The ingredients must be finely ground so that they can be kneaded and blended completely. After kneading, the mixture is put into a ceramic jar, sealed, and buried in the wet ground. The moist mixture must be aged at least three years; generally speaking, the longer the aging process, the richer the resulting fragrance.

The process used to make nerikoh is relatively time-consuming, because if jinkoh wood (all koh contain some jinkoh) were ground by machine, the heat from the machine might cause the wood to lose some of its fragrance. Consequently, grinding, kneading, and forming the dough into small balls must all be done by hand.

In the making of blended incense, measuring the proper amount of each ingredient is considered to be the most difficult step. Subtle variations in fragrance depend crucially on the kind and amount of each ingredient blended. The jinkoh in Shoyeido's joss stick *Shokaku* (正覚) is nearly one hundred percent kyara, whereas *Shunkoh* (春光) contains less expensive kinds of jinkoh.

Furthermore, the fragrance of each ingredient varies depending on the season that it is burned, whether the wood was in the sun or in the shade, the moisture in the air when the blending was done, and so forth. Since many factors influence the final result, each nerikoh is unique. It is not surprising that manufacturers' recipes for the blends and their production methods are closely guarded company secrets today. Some companies even use codes for the blends.

The secrecy surrounding the blending of incense goes back to Heian times. As an example, in the chapter entitled "Umegae" (Plum Branch) in *The Tale of Genji*, Lady Murasaki writes:

> *Setting up his headquarters in the main hall, apart from Murasaki [Genji's consort], Genji turned with great concentration to blending two perfumes according to formulas which—How can they have come into his hands?—had been handed down in secret from the day of the Emperor Nimmyo. In a deeply curtained room . . .*

As is true with today's perfume industry, incense fragrances have become the unmistakable trademark of their manufacturers.

Senkoh 線香 (Joss-Stick Blended Incense)

Joss-stick incense originated in India before the Buddha was born. It consists of a bamboo stick surrounded by blended incense, and resembles a lollipop. Besides imparting fragrance, it measured time, since the incense burned at a constant rate. Only after the Buddha's death did its use in Buddhist rituals become common. The techniques used to make joss sticks were introduced to Japan about 400 years ago. The Japanese version does not have a bamboo stick. Although it is often thought that joss-stick incense was used primarily on Buddhist altars, it has actually been burned purely for the sake of appreciation for just as long.

The length and the fragrance of the joss sticks differ depending on their intended use. Traditional home uses include: 1) for the altar, 2) for listening, and 3) for scenting a room. Stick lengths range from 14 cm to 18 cm (5-1/2 inches to 7 inches). The duration of burning depends on the stick's length and diameter, but the average 14 cm joss stick burns for about twenty to twenty-five minutes, while an 18 cm piece lasts about fifty minutes to an hour. (The part of the stick that is placed in the ashes or in an incense holder remains unburnt.)

Temple joss sticks are used for Buddhist rituals, including meditation. Since they are meant to burn throughout the entire ritual, they are usually longer than the home variety. Some are as long as 73 cm (29 inches), and burn for approximately eight hours.

The ingredients for joss sticks include powdered jinkoh, Japanese Judas tree (Cercidiphyllum japonicum) bark, cloves, camphor, and ambergris. Seven to fifteen ingredients may be blended, all combinations slightly different from nerikoh. Just as eggs are used to bind dry ingredients in dough for baking, the ground bark's gluelike consistency serves to bind the powdered incense. This binding ingredient cannot have a strong smell, and the bark of the Japanese Judas tree serves the purpose well.

To make the joss sticks, all of the ingredients are carefully measured and blended. (The grinding and blending are the most critical parts of the joss-stick manufacturing process as imperfections will cause the joss sticks to warp or unsatisfactorily burn.) Hot water is added and the mixture is kneaded. Sometimes a coloring additive is included to differentiate between blends, and the dough is then pressed through small holes. The result is a spaghetti-like incense, which a skilled worker must carefully guide onto a tray with a bamboo spatula. Approximately 400 sticks are packed into one tray at a time. The trays are then set aside to dry. Care must be taken not to leave any spaces between the sticks to prevent uneven drying and warping. The sticks are left to dry naturally in a temperature-maintained drying room for three to four days. A too damp room will promote fungus growth. Today, machine drying is considered to be more reliable and cost-effective.

What you smell after opening a box of joss sticks is quite different from the fragrance that the sticks will have when they are burning. Usually, the higher the quality of joss stick (the more kyara-quality jinkoh that it contains), the subtler the fragrance before burning. To get the optimum fragrance from the lit joss stick, keep it 20 to 30 cm (8 to 12 inches) away from your nose. The red spot where the stick is burning does not emit the fragrance, rather it is the part of the stick a few millimeters below where the heat causes the fragrance to be released.

Ensuikoh 円錐香 (Blended-Incense Cones)

The manufacturing process for cones is almost identical to that for joss-stick incense. Instead of being pressed through thin holes, however, the kneaded dough is pressed into cone-shaped molds. From about the 1960s, the cones began to be exported in large numbers, because they could be shipped without breakage, unlike joss sticks, which tended to be too fragile. They burn cleanly, in that the ashes do not fall and scatter like joss sticks. Packaging techniques have advanced, and there are few problems with shipping joss sticks over long distances today. Nevertheless, cone-shaped incense remains popular, both abroad and in Japan. *Ensuikoh* customarily is available in floral and citrus fragrances.

Nioi-bukuro 匂い袋 (Sachets)

Rather than being mixed into a dough to be dried and burned, the ground incense ingredients are sometimes placed into a decorative cloth or paper bag, called *nioi-bukuro*. Such sachets are used to scent garments, rooms, and furniture. Some nioi-bukuro are useful as insect repellents, somewhat like moth balls. Nioi-bukuro are often placed in a dresser drawer or in the sleeves of a kimono, or are worn around one's neck. Some nioi-bukuro of larger size or stronger-smelling ingredients may be hung in a room. In addition to emitting a pleasant aroma, the nioi-bukuro—the Japanese people once believed—protects a room from ill fortune. Since they are not heated or burned, they are clean to use, emitting a subtle fragrance for about one year.

While Heian courtiers had to make their own fragrances, we are fortunate now to be able to select from a wide variety of high-quality, ready-made fragrances. Joss-stick incense, coil incense (similar to stick incense, but dried in a coil shape), and cone incense, all of which are the most popular forms of incense in use in Japan today, are now easily obtained outside Japan. The spherically shaped nerikoh incense, which is often used in the tea ceremony, as well as the incense mixtures for sachets mentioned earlier, may in the near future also become easily available abroad. Indeed, there are enough varieties and forms and grades of incense now on the market to please almost any taste. Nowadays, one can even purchase an electric burner for use with incense-wood pieces, eliminating the trouble of having to prepare charcoal and ashes.

Look for Japanese incense in Japan in up-market department stores; stationery shops offering Japanese paper (*washi*), tea ceremony and calligraphy accoutrements; stores specializing in Buddhist artifacts, and, of course, in incense shops. Outside of Japan koh products may be found in Japanese and Oriental specialty shops, although it is probably easiest to order by mail through Shoyeido Corporation in the U.S. (see chapter VII "Sampling Incense Yourself"). Although space does not permit inclusion of a shopper's guide to Japanese incense, price is a good indication of the quality. The higher the percentage of jinkoh contained in a koh product, the higher the price and more refined the fragrance.

IV
The Koh-do Way of Appreciating Incense

Koh-do is different from other contemporary Japanese art forms, such as the tea ceremony and flower arrangement, in that it evolved in close connection with literary pursuits. In Koh-do, there are basically two ways to enjoy the koh (traditionally incense wood, not joss-stick or nerikoh incense). One is to heat a piece of incense in a censer the size of a teacup and let the fragrance permeate the room. The second way is to prepare several pieces for burning, but to enjoy the fragrances in a special context, often literary; this way involves the incense games called *kumikoh* in which two or more kinds of incense are used. A few games are introduced later in this chapter for you to try when you feel ready.

KUMIKOH 組香

Kumikoh are a form of intellectual diversion in the appreciation of incense. By way of comparison, take the case of a musical composition. After seeing a spectacular sunset, a musically inclined person might sit down and compose a piece of music to express his or her impressions of the sky. The work appears on a piece of paper with musical notes that would be played on one or more instruments. Similarly, a person who has studied incense could compose a kumikoh based on the sunset; the composition would be written out in words and played with various kinds of incense. But here the similarity ends. The kumikoh composer only provides the title—a reference to the occasion or literary piece that was the inspiration—and an indication of how many kinds of incense ought to be burned and in what order. Indeed, the composer plays a rather mechanical role. The real interpretation of the game is left in the hands of the master of the incense ceremony, who actually selects the specific kinds of incense to be enjoyed. Such freedom is given to this person in part because it is so difficult to specify precisely the kind of incense that should be used. The kyara used by one master of ceremonies may be closer to the manaban of another. In other words, the sunset now can be played in many ways, depending on the interpretations of the master of the incense ceremony.

It is only in the past few decades that Koh-do has regained the kind of popularity that it enjoyed during the

Edo period. With the increased numbers of students and teachers, the two major schools of Koh-do, Shino and Oie, have now branched off into smaller schools located in various parts of Japan. Although the two schools have some differences in style and emphasis, they agree that the appreciation of incense is of central importance. You do not have to be experienced in Koh-do to appreciate incense. As long as you have a nose and interest, you can enjoy Koh-do from the very first moment simply by listening to and enjoying the incense that has been prepared.

Many kumikoh in the standard repertoire of incense schools are similar and are based on a Japanese poetic form known as the *waka*, which is composed of five lines with the following number of syllables in sequence: 5–7–5–7–7. Other kumikoh are based on images taken from a certain tale, seasonal events, and special occasions. The number of games in existence number into the hundreds, and they range from games for beginners to those for advanced players. Students are first required to be able to identify the characteristics of the six categories of incense fragrances as well as to master the basic games. Later, they acquire the skills necessary to conduct a ceremony, but only after learning how to establish the proper temperature for heating the charcoal, how to cover the charcoal with ashes, and how to form the ashes into an aesthetically pleasing and functional shape that allows the charcoal to maintain access to oxygen and continue burning throughout the ceremony. Students must eventually learn the proper handling of the Koh-do utensils, understand many kumikoh, and be able to select the appropriate fragrances from among the various incense woods. For example, the experienced master of ceremonies will often select very different or very similar fragrances depending on the experience and sophistication of the participants, as well as fragrances that reflect his or her interpretation of the game, while keeping in mind the original composer's intentions.

The majority of these games date back to the heyday of Koh-do in the seventeenth and eighteenth centuries. The Oie School has added new games in this century related to classic literature in response to the late master's encouragement, but the main emphasis continues to be on the appreciation of the delicate fragrance of jin.

There are no rules about students having to learn other Japanese arts in order to advance in Koh-do, though in practice students do study them. Records of the games are written on a sheet of rice paper with a brush, so calligraphy is useful. Some games require participants to compose a poem. Thus, familiarity with certain Japanese literary works and episodes in history is necessary to appreciate some of these games.

In addition to literature and history, students who decide to seriously undertake the practice of Koh-do learn a great deal about art as they study incense utensils. Incense paraphernalia range from simple porcelain incense burners to exquisitely lacquered incense boxes inlaid with mother of pearl. Study and appreciation of such craftsmanship is not the sort of thing one can master in a short period of time, but there is a lot to offer a student with a curious mind.

There are only a few Koh-do textbooks available in contemporary Japanese. Most were prepared during the height of Koh-do and composed in classical Japanese—written in the flowing cursive style of calligraphy which makes them exceedingly difficult for modern Japanese to read or understand. Part of the reason for the paucity of textbooks or other materials on this art form is that the masters surrounded their teachings with an aura of secrecy, as mentioned earlier, by transmitting the art's fine points only verbally to their immediate and carefully selected successors. Fortunately, for an individual to enjoy incense, only a few utensils are necessary: a burner and the tools to handle the ashes and charcoal (not the kind of charcoal used for barbecues but an odorless charcoal especially suited for this purpose). You can buy sets of burners, charcoal, and utensils at shops which specialize in incense. (See appendix for information on how to prepare a censer and utensils for the incense ceremony.)

ART OBJECTS FOR INCENSE 香道具

In Japan, many notable museums have displays of incense paraphernalia. Beautiful lacquered boxes, which would hold all the basic tools for incense ceremonies, called *jisshu-koh-bako,* were produced during the Edo period and were often included in bridal dowry. In the past, traditional Japanese craftsmen liked to fashion incense burners and *jyu-koh-go*, small containers to keep pieces of incense wood or blended incense, and these continue to be popular today. They come in a variety of shapes and designs, in lacquer, ceramic, cloisonné, and silver. In addition to the more standard implements, there are many utensils that resemble toys and are designed to be used in particular kumikoh that are modeled after horse races and archery contests. Suffice it to say that a detailed treatment of incense paraphernalia could easily fill another book!

Let us now see how an incense ceremony is conducted. The following brief description will give you ideas on how to improvise your own incense games. (Substitution ideas for hard-to-find implements are given in the appendix.)

THE INCENSE CEREMONY 香席

Ordinarily, the room used for an incense ceremony holds ten comfortably: a master of ceremonies, a record-keeper, and eight participants. The room is usually the size of ten *tatami* (straw mats), or approximately 16 feet by 13 feet, and the participants sit in the Japanese style on the mat flooring with legs folded underneath. (A typical seating arrangement is shown in the appendix; see "Traditional Room Layout and Seating Arrangement for the Incense Ceremony.") Participants, beginning with the guest of honor, sit clockwise from the master of ceremonies for the Shino School and counterclockwise for the Oie School. (Elderly participants are often invited to sit in the honored place.) When the participants are seated, the master and the record-keeper enter the room. The former carries a wooden box containing the necessary paraphernalia—utensils, incense selected by the master of ceremonies and wrapped beforehand, and incense burners—and the latter a wooden table, record sheets, answer sheets, a box containing ink, an inkstone, and brushes. Beforehand, a stack of smaller flat boxes, each with inkstone and a brush for the guests to write their answers, has been placed to the right of the guest of honor's seat to be passed around to the participants after the ceremony has begun. If the ceremony is for experienced students of Koh-do, there will usually be no detailed explanation of the game to be played except for its title, although often the master of ceremonies may greet the participants and explain the theme of the game and its procedure as a matter of formality. This is because only the actual incense is changed with each playing of a kumikoh, while the theme and interpretations remain the same.

The master of ceremonies bows and unfolds a placemat-like sheet, places it on the tatami, and transfers the objects from his box onto the sheet. The sequence of transfer and position of each object is fixed according to age-old rules. The utensils which are used to handle incense pieces are ritually cleaned. The master once more checks that everything is in order, making sure that the charcoal is emitting a steady heat and that the ash covering the charcoal is shaped neatly. (See appendix: "Shino Incense Censer.") Meanwhile, the record-keeper writes down the title of the game, the names and kinds of incense selected for the occasion, and the participants' names. At the end of the game he or she will record the participants' answers on the same sheets. Both the master and the record-keeper conduct and participate in the game, while making sure that the proper charcoal temperature is maintained and that the fragrance is being steadily emitted.

Now the kumikoh begins. Let us use the game called

Shirakawa-koh (Shirakawa Border Station) as an example. (Concise instructions for this game appear under "Sample Kumikoh for Fun" in the next section.) Shirakawa-koh is based on a poem written by the poet Noin of the late Heian period.

> *Miyako o ba*
> *Kasumi to tomo ni*
> *Ideshika zo*
> *Akikaze zo fuku*
> *Shirakawa no seki*

> I left the capital,
> Veiled in spring mist.
> An autumn wind blows here,
> At Shirakawa Border station.

Although the notion of going on a trip across the country may not seem so significant to us, we should remember that in ancient times traveling was much more difficult. The distance from Kyoto to Shirakawa is more than 600 kilometers (370 miles), and required many months traveling by foot. It was rare for most people to travel more than a few miles from where they were born, and such a long journey was easily one of the most significant events in a person's life.

The three kinds of jinkoh used in this game (any three may be selected) are called: *Mist in the Capital, Autumn Wind,* and *Shirakawa Border Station.* Prior to the ceremony, the master of ceremonies has cut two pieces each of *Mist in the Capital* and *Autumn Wind* and wrapped them individually, marking each packet for his or her exclusive identification. (See appendix: "Wrapping Incense for Kumikoh.") One piece of *Mist in the Capital* and one of *Autumn Wind* are used as samples (heated in a censer and passed around, beginning with the guest in the honored place). The master of ceremonies identifies these samples for the participants. Participants memorize the two fragrances to identify the third unsampled fragrance. (There is only one piece of *Shirakawa Border Station,* also wrapped in a small packet.)

When the sampling is completed, the master shuffles the three packets, one each of *Mist in the Capital, Autumn Wind,* and *Shirakawa Border Station.* As the master of ceremonies is doing this, the guest of honor now passes the stack of boxes containing the inkstones and brushes to the person beside him or her. Each participant takes a box and passes the stack on to the next participant. The master of ceremonies then passes the three pieces of incense in random order for the participants to listen to and identify. (Since the master of ceremonies was responsible for wrapping the incense in packets in the first place, he or she can easily identify each one.) The master of ceremonies listens first, making sure that the fragrance is emitting steadily before passing the censer on to the honored guest. (The master of ceremonies participates in listening to the fragrances and "identifying" them as a matter of protocol.) The participants write the names of the fragrances on their answer sheet in the order in which they listen to them. (See appendix: "Participant's Answer Sheet for Kumikoh.") It is important to note that the results of participants' performances are not scored in the usual sense. The idea of the game—of all kumikoh—is to enjoy the process of listening to the fragrances and, in this particular game, to retrace the long journey the poet took many years ago. The poet Noin spent two full seasons covering a distance that now takes no more than a few hours by bullet train. When the poet left the capital it was still spring, but by the time he arrived at his destination it was autumn.

When all the answer sheets are turned in and the scribe has completed the transcription of the answers on the master record sheet, the master of ceremonies reads the correct identifications. The record-keeper checks the answers submitted by the participants, and then offers these interpretations:

- For all fragrances correctly identified: Crossed the Border
- All fragrances incorrectly identified: Stopped at the Border
- Only *Spring Mist* correctly identified: Spring Wind
- Only *Autumn Wind* correctly identified: Fallen Leaves
- Only *Shirakawa Border Station* correctly identified: Travel Garments.

When the complete record sheet is passed around for the participants to examine, everyone sees how they fared during their "travels," compared to the other journeyers. (This is done while the master of ceremonies "cleans up," enlisting the record-keeper's help in gathering the paraphernalia and taking everything back to the preparation room or kitchen.) Some safely reached the destination; some were stopped at the border by unsympathetic officials; others traveled slowly, or reached the destination when the leaves were all gone; and perhaps one traveler got only as far as folding his or her travel garments! The master of ceremonies and the record-keeper return to their places and ask the guests how they enjoyed the game, then give the record sheet to the participant who identified the most number of fragrances correctly. Everyone bows, to thank each other for the enjoyable time spent sharing fragrances together and to signify the end of the ceremony.

If you have the opportunity to attend an incense ceremony, here are some helpful hints: try to physically and mentally prepare yourself for appreciating the subtle fragrances of incense. For your own sake, and of course for fellow participants as well, don't eat anything spicy or wear any perfume or strong deodorant prior to attending a ceremony. Clean socks (without holes!) are also recommended. If possible, go on an empty stomach. You probably won't listen to incense as well if you have just eaten.

You may notice that the alcoves of a room used for the incense ceremony are decorated with a scroll or two, or other objects associated with incense, but seldom with flowers or plants, particularly fragrant ones. This is so that no fragrance other than the incense will permeate the room. Even if they do not have strong smells, flowers and plants are usually temporarily placed elsewhere as simplicity and emptiness are considered more conducive to listening to a subtle fragrance, and blank space sometimes gives the maximum "room" for imagination. Of course, you can appreciate incense in any kind of room of any size, although if there is a strong draft the fragrance will be that much more difficult to listen to. Unlike for the tea ceremony, therefore, having an incense ceremony outside is not practical.

A word about how to hold a censer with a mica plate and incense chip may be helpful. There are slight differences between the Shino and Oie schools, as below.

The utmost care must be paid to holding the censer upright so that the incense chip on the mica plate will not slip into the ashes. (Usually the incense chip is more likely to slip than the mica plate into the ashes.) Once the chip gets covered with ashes, it will not heat properly and the fragrance will be marred. Needless to say, it becomes a mess for the master of ceremonies to clean, and it is not appropriate to use another piece for the rest of the group as each piece is likely to smell subtly different!

Pick up the entire censer with the right hand (left-handed persons do the opposite) and place it on the left-hand palm. In the Shino School style, secure the censer by placing the left thumb on the lip. In the Oie School style, the censer cup is deeper, so the thumb is not placed on the lip at all. Cup the right hand over the censer opening, leaving a small "o"-shaped opening to inhale the fragrance. Put your nose close to the opening and inhale a few times gently. Turn your head and exhale away from the censer so as not to blow the chip off the mica or scatter

Photo by Ikko Nagano

the ashes. Since the wood chip is very small in size, each guest listens two or three times and passes the censer on to the next guest. That's all.

SAMPLE KUMIKOH FOR FUN

Shirakawa-koh 白河香 (Shirakawa Border Station)

Many of the kumikoh games have a seasonal theme. This particular kumikoh recreates a journey taken by the priest Noin during his journey approximately 800 years ago. Traveling a distance of only several hundred miles was both a physical and emotional undertaking, requiring an altogether different kind of preparation, since rapid transportation such as we have today was non-existent. Actually, this is precisely the reason why it is interesting for us to retrace Noin's steps. It takes us away from our own busy lives and allows us to slip back into time, when the pace of living was slower—and perhaps more methodical. The kumikoh was based on the following poem written by the priest:

> *Miyako o ba*
> *Kasumi to tomo ni*
> *Ideshika zo*
> *Akikaze zo fuku*
> *Shirakawa no seki*

> I left the capital,
> Veiled in spring mist.
> An autumn wind blows here,
> At Shirakawa Border Station.

Incense: Three kinds

1. *Miyako no kasumi* (**Mist in the Capital**)
   Two pieces wrapped individually (one is a sample).
2. *Akikaze* (**Autumn Wind**)
   Two pieces wrapped individually (one is a sample).
3. *Shirakawa no seki* (**Shirakawa Border Station**)
   One piece wrapped (no sample).

Listening:

Step 1. The master of ceremonies informs the guests that the three pieces of incense are called *Mist in the Capital*, *Autumn Wind*, and *Shirakawa Border Station*. Guests listen to the two sample incense pieces, *Mist in the Capital* first, and *Autumn Wind* second.

Step 2. The master of ceremonies shuffles the three pieces (one each of *Mist in the Capital*, *Autumn Wind*, and *Shirakawa Border Station*).

Step 3. After the burning of each incense piece, guests indicate their listening by writing down the names of the incense on the answer sheet provided.

Interpreting the Answers:

The following remarks are recorded.

∫∫∫ All correct: Crossed the Border

∫ Only *Mist in the Capital* correct: Spring Wind

∫ Only *Autumn Wind* correct: Fallen Leaves

∫ Only *Shirakawa Border Station* correct: Travel Garments

None correct: Stopped at Shirakawa Border Station

Appreciation:

It is time for the participants to relax and review how

well they traveled. Some traveled far and successfully crossed the border station. Some were not accustomed to traveling on foot and did not go very far before they decided to return to the capital and enjoy spring. Some traveled, but it was almost winter when they arrived at their destination. Some have strong memories of their experiences at the border station, where the officials were hard on them and made the crossing difficult. Some were only able to go as far as preparing their travel garments. No matter what stage of the journey the participants reached, it was fun. Everyone is a winner in this game. What is important is that participants have had a chance to make a journey in a different time, together through a sensory mode.

Sanshu-koh 三種香 (Game of Three)

When studying the piano, the diligent music student will no doubt spend many hours practicing scales. *Sanshu-koh* is a scales-practicing version of an incense game for Koh-do. There are no seasonal themes, nor are poetic names assigned to fragrances. You concentrate on identifying the differences and similarities among the six basic fragrances of koh.

Incense: Three kinds

Three pieces each of three kinds of incense, for a total of nine pieces, are wrapped individually in packets. They are shuffled well, then three are randomly selected to be prepared for listening.

Listening:

Step 1. The master of ceremonies informs the guests that the three pieces of incense are called **1, 2,** and **3** in the order presented.

Step 2. After the burning of each incense piece, guests indicate their listening by drawing three vertical lines on the answer sheet provided. The right line is for the first piece to which they have listened, the middle line for the second piece, and the left line for the third piece. ⁽³⁾⁽²⁾⁽¹⁾ |||

Step 3. Guests indicate incense possessing the same fragrance by connecting the vertical lines at the top with a horizontal one (example: ⊓|). If incense pieces are not the same, the lines remain unconnected (|||).

Interpreting the Answers:

||| Evergreen trees

Ⅲ Snow on a lonely peak

Ⅲ Dew on pampas grass

ⅠⅢ Plum blossoms from the neighbor's house

ⅢⅠ Sound of the *koto*

Appreciation:

This game is a simpler version of *Genji-koh*, which calls for five vertical lines and is explained further on. The five poetic appellations are not necessarily derived pictographically from the patterns, so there is really nothing to ponder. The aim of the game is simply to enjoy the fragrance of the three pieces of incense and the individual patterns that are created. (At the end of the game, the master of ceremonies will share with the participants the correct order of incense burnt.) Once each incense piece is prepared, it may be passed around as many as three times so that everyone can feel comfortable identifying the fragrance.

The patterns here have traditional Japanese appellations. These designations may seem removed from the experiences of most of us, so it may be fun to devise new ones that better reflect our feelings for nature and our daily lives.

Sankei-koh 三景香 (The Three Scenic Spots)

There is virtually no Japanese person who cannot name "The Three Scenic Spots" of Japan: Matsushima, Amanohashidate, and Itsukushima. It is not certain when they were designated as scenic spots, but by the beginning of the Edo Period (1600–1868) they were already famous. There is a popular story about Basho, Japan's greatest haiku poet who, when first setting eyes on Matsushima, threw his brush away, uttering "Matsushima! Ah, Matsushima! Matsushima!" Such was its overwhelming beauty.

The scenic attractions of these coastal spots are man-made as well as natural. Matsushima consists of over 260 small pine-covered islands off the coast of Sendai. Amanohashidate, near Kyoto, is a white sandbar approximately 3.3 kilometers (2 miles) long that stretches across peaceful Miyazu bay and is dotted with many picturesque, twisted pine trees. Itsukushima island is set off by a large vermilion *torii* gate in the Inland Sea, which beckons worshippers to the sacred shrine compounds.

This kumikoh encourages you to imagine a boat ride to each of these scenic spots.

Incense: Four kinds

1. *Matsushima*

Two pieces wrapped individually (one is a sample).

2. *Amanohashidate*
   Two pieces wrapped individually (one is a sample).
3. *Itsukushima*
   Two pieces wrapped individually (one is a sample).
4. *Boat*
   One piece wrapped (no sample).

Listening:

Step 1: Guests listen to the three sample incense pieces in the following order: *Matsushima*, *Amanohashidate*, and *Itsukushima*.

Step 2: The master of ceremonies shuffles the remaining four packets.

Step 3: Guests listen to the randomly ordered four pieces of incense, recording their answers after each scent.

Interpreting the Answers:

The following remarks are recorded.

∫∫∫∫ Four correct: The Three Scenic Spots
∫∫   Two correct: Evening Mist
∫   One correct: Morning Mist
∫★ One correct (*Boat*): View
None correct: Cloud of Mist

Appreciation:

No one can be incorrect, since the purpose of the game is to enjoy the scenic spots. If your answer sheet reads: **Matsushima**, **Itsukushima**, **Boat**, and **Amanohashidate**, it is interpreted that you have visited Matsushima and Itsukushima, and Amanohashidate is the next spot for which the boat is heading. Only a poetic grading makes sense, so for those who actually identified two, it is interpreted that the scenic spots were somewhat obscured by the evening mist. If a participant gets only one correct answer, it is because of the morning mist, which lingers longer than the evening mist and thus obscures the scenery further. However, if the one correct is **Boat**, then the player can be said to have viewed the spots from the boat, without having actually set foot on land. And of course the mist at times can be as thick as clouds, in which case nothing can be seen.

This game can be adapted to reflect regional scenic spots. For a gathering of lovers of the Hawaiian islands, three kinds of incense might be selected to represent, say, the islands of Maui, Kauai, and Hawaii, and a fourth kind of incense to represent an outrigger canoe.

Genji-koh 源氏香 (The Tale of Genji)
Many kumikoh are based on Japanese literary sources such

as classical legends, tales, and poems, with the majority taking their themes from the latter. The most popular kumikoh is *The Tale of Genji*, or *Genji-koh*, although most Japanese people do not know that such a game even exists. Yet the symbolic patterns used in this game are familiar to many, since they are used as designs on kimono and lacquerware.

Incense: Five kinds

Five pieces each of five kinds of incense, for a total of twenty-five pieces individually wrapped in small packets.

Listening:

Step 1: The master of ceremonies shuffles the twenty-five packets and randomly selects five, setting aside the remaining twenty packets.

Step 2: The master of ceremonies shuffles the five packets.

Step 3: Guests listen to the five pieces, recording their answers on the answer sheet after each. Their answers are not written in words, but indicated with five vertical lines. The same fragrances are indicated by connecting the vertical lines with a horizontal line on the top. The line on the far right represents the first scent, the second line the second scent and so forth on to the far left, which represents the fifth scent. If the first and the second are the same, and the rest are all different fragrances, then the pattern would look like this: |||∏

Each resulting *Genji-koh* pattern corresponds to a particular chapter from *The Tale of Genji*.

Interpreting the Answers:

Fifty-two different patterns are possible using twenty-five pieces of five different kinds of incense. Refer to the list of emblems provided for the corresponding chapter titles.

Appreciation:

If a guest's answer is completely correct, then it is indicated by the character 玉, a five-stroke character meaning "jewel" or "gem." This is because the character of Prince Genji was regarded as a beautiful "gem." Although a guest might interpret a scent differently and record a "wrong" answer, this should not be a reason for disappointment. It simply means that the participant read or listened to a different chapter. (*The Tale of Genji* is originally meant to be read, of course, but in our incense game, we listen to it.) We repeat this four more times, listening to a random selection of five pieces of incense each session, which can be done on the same day or on four different days.

EMBLEMS

THE BOOK OF INCENSE

THE BOOK OF INCENSE

THE BOOK OF INCENSE

THE BOOK OF INCENSE

V

The Pleasures of
Incense Today

When courtiers in *The Tale of Genji* speak of special kimono sleeves scented with incense, it sounds very romantic. But in those days baths were not easily taken, so fragrances were used to mask body odor. Washing one's hair was no small undertaking, and consequently incense pillows were popular. Fortunately, we don't need to use incense in this way today—we can play and have fun with fragrances.

Bringing incense into one's daily life is not as exotic an activity as it may seem. It is done as easily as playing music, arranging flowers, preparing tea or coffee, or taking a bath. After all, fragrance is already an inseparable part of contemporary daily life. You will find sources of fragrance everywhere: soaps, balsam in dressers and closets, potpourri, scented candles, handkerchiefs, gloves, writing paper and envelopes, and of course, the aromas of cooking and baking. If you can select flowers to send to family and friends, using the colors, shapes, and fragrance of the flowers to help communicate your feelings, and choose perfumes to suit your feelings and the occasion, then you can most certainly enjoy incense.

Recently, several major Japanese building companies and a steel company have created freshly scented working environments by piping various fragrances through ventilation systems—something like muzak for the nose. Fragrances such as lemon or cedar reportedly resulted in a considerable improvement in the office environment and worker performance. Results of research conducted by cosmetic giant Shiseido show that lemon helps employees keep alert, a floral fragrance aids concentration, cedar relieves fatigue, cinnamon lifts one's spirits, and jasmine reduces anxiety. Initial concern that such fragrances might clash with an individual's cologne or perfume, or be an invasion of "smell privacy" if they proved to be disagreeable, has been put to rest. The truth is, the scents are on such a subtle level that many people are unconscious of their presence. When used with consideration, moderation, and respect for others, aroma has been shown to be quite pleasing and beneficial, as Japanese companies with scent programs are beginning to prove.

Whereas some incense ingredients and spices have been used for only practical applications, such as to protect clothes from bugs and to mask odors, other ingredients may enhance one's imagination or enrich one's feelings. Incense can also have a tranquilizing effect. In Japan, some doctors burn incense for patients with psychological problems. In the United States and elsewhere, aromatherapists and other healers use incense or aromatic oils for a variety of ailments.

Zen monks use incense for meditation as well as for rituals. Even if one is not a monk, a subtle aroma of incense in the air, rather than the various smells associated with daily life at home and at work (including smells of family and colleagues), does help one to concentrate. We all live our lives in the here and now, but at the same time we often long for freedom from the rigid structure of civilization. The mundane world in which we live and work has become so fraught with pressures that even its smells can make us tense. Listening to the fragrances of incense gives us the opportunity to become larger than our busy minds, because they are so fundamentally simple, subtle, and thoroughly comforting.

Incense wood, besides providing enormous pleasure as a fragrance, can also be displayed as an ornament, though one should remember that high-quality incense can cost almost as much as gold. A rice-grain-size piece of kyara wood that we burn can cost a dollar or so. Some "antique pieces" are like heirloom treasures—and priceless in this respect. But collecting various kinds of aromatic wood, especially jinkoh, can be enjoyable in the same way as building up a collection of wines. Some naturally formed pieces of aromatic wood are beautiful for their shapes and colors. There exists the pleasure of imagining the original tree growing in a tropical jungle, and its mysterious history: decay to transformation to aromatic substance. After many years, it is unearthed and brought to us, and then, as we cut off a small piece and indulge in its fragrance, we somehow transcend our mortal existence. We indirectly experience a distant and exotic place many lifetimes in the past. It is like tasting a distinguished, very old red wine (although incense wood is much older and does not age better or become worse with time), or looking at the concentric circles of a giant redwood tree stump, contemplating its awesome age.

If you have the opportunity to own a piece of jinkoh, you can even give it a name. What kind of image did you get when you listened to its fragrance? Was it something like clouds sailing across a big bright moon? You could name it, for example, *Moon River*. Or *Crossing the Moon*.

If you smelled something profoundly sweet, you may want to call it **Vermilion**. Or even after a special person. It is entirely up to you. For a piece taken out of a larger piece, you can keep the same name as the large piece or give different names to every piece you cut off.

Opportunities for burning or using incense on a daily basis abound. For example, in entertaining. A small piece of incense wood (or joss stick) can be burning in the hallway or living room shortly before your first guests arrive to create a relaxing, hospitable atmosphere and to stimulate the appetite. (See appendix: "Using Incense to Scent a Room.")

Keeping a sachet or two in your dresser drawers and closets will work to give your clothes a signature scent. When you put these garments on, and they are warmed by your body heat, the fragrance may subtly vary each time the garment is worn. Women can keep a sachet in their purse. There are also pretty hanging sachets made of brocaded fabrics and some incense comes in colorful bags and baskets. All make attractive, fragrant ornaments.

The various kinds of readily available incense are beguiling, but it's also rewarding to create your own fragrances.

The nobles in the Heian court, after making their own *nerikoh* incense, often gave it as gifts. Since there was no commercially made incense at that time, every piece had to be homemade and blended according to recipes, either brought from China or modified. Similar to cakes and pies that are prepared and baked separately, each blend of incense came out slightly different.

Shoyeido now offers a kit for making nerikoh incense at home. After making your incense you can name your handmade creations and select unique containers to burn it in.

You can make your own sachets by selecting fabric you like, sewing it into pouches, and filling the pouches with sachet refills (which come in simple paper bags). The sachets do not even have to be in the shape of a pouch— they can be cut and sewn in any shape you desire.

Joss-stick incense, on the other hand, is not something you can easily make yourself, so it's best to leave it to the incense companies. As explained previously, its manufacture requires a great deal of experience, not to mention proper tools and machines. Besides, there are already numerous kinds of joss-stick incense available, and many ways to enjoy it.

In the next chapter I will give some suggestions on how to creatively enjoy incense, which should help you to come up with your own interesting games for experiencing koh.

Art forms such as the tea ceremony, flower arrangement, archery, singing, calligraphy, and incense ceremony are often called *okeikogo* (taking lessons) or *asobi* (play). *Asobi*, however, does not simply mean an extravagant pastime for the rich or something in which only children can engage. Far from it. People must have found some meaning in the training they underwent for Koh-do and other Ways to have preserved these traditional art forms for us to enjoy today. What, then, is the value and significance of activities that we ordinarily call *asobi* or play?

Dutch historian Johan Huizinga writes in *Homo Ludens* that the reasons for play include "discharging superabundant energy," "relaxing after exertion," "training for the demands of life," "compensating for unfulfilled longing," and acting on "an innate urge to exercise a certain faculty." But Huizinga states that, as with children who take their playing so seriously that they eventually step out of reality (or confuse the world of play with that of reality), play can be serious and may even rise to heights of beauty and the sublime. Play casts a spell over us; it is "enchanting" and "captivating" and brings us "to rhythm and harmony." Does this seem familiar?

Asobi enriches our lives by allowing us to grow mentally. The practice of the Way of Koh, as *asobi*, provides an exercise in *sense-ability*, or mental expansion. In many ways, it also offers us healthful benefits. In this regard, a Zen priest in the sixteenth century is believed to have written that there are ten virtues that incense holds:

1. *It brings communication with the transcendent.*
2. *It purifies mind and body.*
3. *It removes uncleanliness.*
4. *It keeps one alert.*
5. *It can be a companion in the midst of solitude.*
6. *In the midst of busy affairs, it brings a moment of peace.*
7. *When it is plentiful, one never tires of it.*
8. *When there is little, still one is satisfied.*
9. *Age does not change its efficacy.*
10. *Used everyday, it does no harm.*

Though many centuries have passed and our lives are different from those of people in the sixteenth century, these ten virtues are applicable in our times. Regardless of the time and place, the type of jinkoh and with whom one burns it, the outcome of listening to incense can be summed up beautifully in the words of Lady Murasaki, author of *The Tale of Genji*:

hito no on-kokochi ito en nari
"One's mind has become elegant."

VI

The Traditional and Modern with Koh

You will often find a Japanese person worried about making a fool of him- or herself at an "incense ceremony." He or she thinks that it is a very serious ritual that must be approached solemnly. Moreover, there is the common misapprehension: "I will have to guess the right fragrances. There is no way I can do that." Perhaps because of the centuries-old protocol and formalized games, the incense ceremony is almost always perceived as a stiff or ritualized ceremony, or as a competition to identify fragrances. Viewed in the true spirit of Koh-do, however, it is really a party to appreciate and play with fragrances.

Being in Japan certainly makes it easier to appreciate koh in the traditional Japanese way. However, for many of those who read this book and who have no easy access to incense ceremonies, stores, and knowledgeable friends, some modification or adaptation may be necessary. For example, a small incense study group in Boston is learning the traditional Japanese ways, but at the same time, new ways more conducive to the Boston environment are being explored. The group has received permission from Shino School Master Sogen Hachiya to modify the ceremonial details, for instance by the use of translated English terms and horizontal writing on the record sheets, and by the substitution of some utensils. You may want to adapt aspects of the incense ceremony further, and modify the kumikoh. A note about this is in order. Many Japanese people respect this old art form as part of their heritage and are probably inclined to preserve it in its present form rather than to modify it to better suit modern tastes. Even the few very advanced students who are allowed to teach by the master of the incense school will not dare change the accepted format or interpretation of an incense game. Perhaps this is how it is when one is part of a school. You, however, are in the enviable position of forming your own informal gathering and modifying the art of the incense ceremony as you please. Perhaps people will say that it is not "Koh-do," but if you are contemplating the fragrances and enjoying them, then at least you have the essential element of the art—the spirit!

Without changing the art drastically (and thus, we hope, not upsetting anyone at the formal schools!) let me suggest some nontraditional ways with Japanese koh. I call this the Modern Way with Koh. From the practical standpoints of accessibility and cost, the easiest way to appreciate incense will be to use joss sticks instead of incense wood (although I highly recommend the experience of Koh-do with incense wood). Fortunately, the traditional way of incense does allow some room to improvise and expand the games with Western materials and into Western contexts, and some themes have already been mentioned in the Koh-do section. Let me suggest an idea or two as a start, and then you may go off on your own.

In terms of games and themes, there is nothing that you cannot do. Even the incense masters, when they interpret the games, do not necessarily have to follow one unique set of rules. Since no one can dictate another's mind, the master of ceremonies cannot control the participants' appreciation. As long as everyone enjoys the fragrance of koh itself, the goal is achieved. Among the traditional games, there are ones that have sports themes such as kickball, horseracing, and archery. But some of these sports-oriented games are less favored over traditional literary games, since the competitive aspects are overemphasized.

I believe the way of appreciating games should change with each generation, and that we ought to be able to appreciate fragrances in a way suitable to our times, while still staying in touch with the ways and manner people had of enjoying incense hundreds of years ago. Some guidelines to keep in mind are: let no one be extravagant or wasteful with the precious incense; the games are not merely for the sake of achieving points and skills; don't forget seasonal appreciation; make the play a source of peace and comfort. Our methods may be different, but the incense does not change. And this incense is the vehicle that connects the present with the past, which is the amazing thing.

SUGGESTION 1. Customizing Interpretations

When playing a traditional kumikoh, there really is not much we can alter, except to change the interpretation of the game. The Koh-do students in Japan follow the suggested interpretations, but we might come up with our own. Take Shirakawa-koh as an example. After having traveled in the priest Noin's steps, and discussing what that experience was like, the participants can then relate his journey to their own travels. You may have had trouble with the border officials when you were traveling from Thailand to Malaysia. Or when you traveled through different seasons in one journey: it was winter in New England, but when you reached your destination in Hawaii, it was summer. How was it going through the security check or agricultural inspection?

Customarily, the time for appreciation is very short: after the game, when the guests look over each other's answers as the record sheet is passed around. Often there is no notable exchange of appreciation or reaction to a game. And, by the time the record sheet has been looked over by everyone present, the master of ceremonies has finished putting the paraphernalia back in the tray and is ready to finish the ceremony by presenting the record sheet to the winning participant. But we may want to set aside an additional ten to fifteen minutes for a free exchange of participants' memories or associations.

SUGGESTION 2. Naming

In the case of joss-stick incense, a box or a stick already has a name given by the manufacturer. If, for some reason, you do not agree with that name, you may wish to rename it with a word that conjures up the image you associate with that particular fragrance.

If you obtained a small piece of aromatic wood, burn a tiny piece, listen, and give it a name. For example, if I listen to a sharp clear smell, and that sharpness comes and goes, I might call it **Moon in the Woods**, because the moon is hidden by the trees here and there. If it is a stubbornly sweet smell, I might name it **Passion**, or **Valentine**. Light sweet smell? Maybe **Spring Breeze**. A dispersed kind of light sweetness? Then maybe **Garland**. And so forth. Have fun using your imagination!

Needless to say, you generally wouldn't want to give a name that is associated with misery, sorrow, or pain, although if you were feeling sad or had experienced a tragedy, you may wish to name the fragrance as an invocation of love, release, or guidance.

SUGGESTION 3. Linked Poem or Short Story

The master of ceremonies offers a fragrance and asks participants to share their images and memories associated with it. Or try a short story or poem created by everyone present. Have one guest begin by writing the opening word or line on a note pad and pass it around for all participants to contribute (a representative could serve as the scribe, recording everyone's thoughts), creating a linked poem or short story. The latter may work well with school children.

SUGGESTION 4. New Games

Try creating a new game!

Mayflower-koh (Created by the Boston Study Group of the Shino School)
The kumikoh, Mayflower-koh, is based on a short

poem by New England poet Emily Dickinson, who spent her entire life in Amherst, Massachusetts. Like all of her poetry, this one has no title; however, those who are familiar with the New England woodlands can easily recognize the subject of the poem to be the Mayflower. This delicate flower first blooms in April, pale and mostly hidden by the decaying leaves of the woodland carpet, and grows more visible by May, its colors having turned an intense pink. In this verse about the Mayflower, the poet helps us to see the beauty and mystery of ordinary things in our daily lives. When the blossom makes its brief appearance, Nature "forswears Antiquity" and is reborn again, new and fresh. This is a welcomed reminder that life continues to regenerate itself. Some of the images in Mayflower-koh come from the poem; other images reach beyond the poem to suggest the experience of the poet, and to suggest one's own private walk in the woods in early spring, which may be filled with discoveries—including, hopefully, the fleeting Mayflower.

Pink—small—and punctual—
Aromatic—low—
Covert—in April—
Candid—in May—

Dear to the Moss—
Known to the Knoll—
Next to the Robin
In every human Soul—
Bold little Beauty
Bedecked with thee
Nature forswears
Antiquity—

Incense: Three kinds

1. *Melting Snow*
   Two pieces wrapped individually (one is a sample).
2. *Snake Sleeping in the Sun*
   Two pieces wrapped individually (one is a sample).
3. *Mayflower*
   One piece (no sample to be offered).

Note: If using joss sticks, you will have to use your creativity in burning them, so that participants will not be able to identify them by their colors.

Listening:

Step 1. The guests listen to the samples of the first two pieces of incense.

Step 2. The master of ceremonies shuffles the remaining three pieces (numbers 1, 2, 3).

Step 3. The guests listen to the randomly ordered three pieces of incense, drawing their identifying symbols after each scent.

The symbols to be used are:

Melting Snow   *Snake Sleeping in the Sun*   *Mayflower*

Step 4. The scribe records the guests' answers, using the same three symbols beside the guests' names.

Interpreting the Answers:

The scribe records the following remarks:

    ∫∫∫ All three correctly identified: "Mayflower"

    ∫ Only one correctly identified: "1"

    None correctly identified: no mark

Appreciation:

If a participant has correctly identified all three fragrances, then he or she had a peaceful walk in the woods, perhaps filled with insights and a successful sighting of the Mayflower. If only **_Melting Snow_** was identified, then the walk was too brief, perhaps because the weather was cold. If only **_Snake Sleeping in the Sun_** was identified, then the walk was taken hurriedly, perhaps for fear of coming upon other snakes. If only **_Mayflower_** was identified, then possibly one discovered the Mayflower quite by accident, not knowing what it was.

VII
Sampling Incense Yourself

Now all you need to do is organize your own incense appreciation gathering. Invite several friends. . . . Even before they arrive, you may want to set the scene by lighting a joss stick from one of the packets that you have bought ahead. Put the incense in the hole of the small holder that came with the incense, or you may wish to place the stick in a container that compliments your room, or that suits your sense of the season and mood. A flat-bottomed cup, dish, or glass is recommended for safety, with a wide rim to better catch the ashes. After your friends arrive and are seated comfortably (try to choose a simply-furnished room), explain that many Japanese joss-stick fragrances are associated with the seasons.

Though people's feelings about and appreciation of the seasons differ, it is helpful to know there are some conventional Japanese words and phrases that are particularly representative of the four seasons, such as names of certain trees, flowers, animals, and foods. Spring is warm and soft, with mornings full of mist, cherry blossoms, and skylarks. In most parts of Japan the summers are hot and humid, and people long for things like water, shade, soft breezes, and simple flowers like morning glories that make them feel cool. Autumn is colorful with maple leaves and fragrant with chrysanthemums, and the long melancholy nights are filled with the chirping of crickets and the changing phases of the moon. The winter's first snow is exciting for children, and the world turns white, silent, and tranquil. People also long for evergreen pines, bamboo, and plum blossoms that thrive even in the severe winter.

Light either side of the first joss stick with a match or a lighter. Shake it gently once or twice to extinguish the flame. Now sit back and listen to the incense. The subtle aroma of this type of high-quality joss-stick incense is best appreciated at a distance of 30 cm (12 inches) or so. Now you and your friends can describe which joss stick goes with which season.

Incense has had a long and rich history both inside and outside of Japan, but this great sense of tradition should not discourage us from experimentation. Indeed, as we have seen, experimentation has been central to the enjoyment of incense in Japan since the Heian Period. Such innovation continues even to this day. For example, it was Shoyeido, one of the oldest incense companies in Japan (whose roots go back to 1705), that introduced the popular cone incense to the West. In addition to incense itself, Shoyeido has been innovative with other incense products; for instance, its new line of modern incense containers and burners called "Lisn" combine traditional and modern aesthetic styles. Tradition and innovation need not be in conflict but may coexist as part of a fine balance.

Shoyeido was founded by Hata Rokubei upon his retirement in 1705. As a man of refined tastes, Hata enjoyed the hobby of blending incense. His successors have all devoted themselves to the art of creating evanescent, delicate fragrances by blending various aromatic spices and ingredients, which are brought to Japan from Southeast Asia.

Businesses in Japan that specialize in traditional Japanese arts and crafts have a tendency to stagnate, and the great-grandfather of the present president of Shoyeido was attentive to this possibility, especially after the Meiji Restoration of 1868 opened the floodgates to Western influences. Hata tried to be as innovative as possible; he created new kinds of incense (including the cone shape) and introduced Japanese koh at the World Exposition held in Chicago in

1894. Only four years later, Shoyeido began exporting sets of incense and burners to America. Hata was thus the first to export incense to the West and a pioneer of incense fragrances that appealed to modern sensibilities. By the late 1920s, about ten years after World War I, Shoyeido was unable to manufacture enough cone incense to meet the demands from overseas.

The company's main office in the center of Kyoto near the Imperial Palace is on the original site of Hata's residential quarters. The original shop was remodeled into a modern five-story building, which has kept the original beams. Once in the general vicinity of the shop, you almost do not need a map, for the mysteriously elegant fragrance in the air will guide you. If you have a chance, it is worth taking a tour of the new ultramodern high-tech factory in Katsura City, a suburb of Kyoto. The three Shoyeido shops located in Kyoto, Tokyo, and Sapporo also have beautiful incense rooms to which people come for lessons. One or two people who can speak English are usually on hand in each shop, but you might want to write or call before your visit just to be sure. If you are lucky, Mr. Masataka Hata, the president of Shoyeido, will be there to entertain you with his fluent English and charming sense of humor.

IN JAPAN:
Shoyeido Incense Company
Karasuma Nijo Agaru
Nakagyo-ku, Kyoto 604-0857
Telephone: 075-212-5590
Fax: 075-212-5595

IN THE U.S.:
Shoyeido Corporation
P.O. Box 18353
Boulder, CO 80308-9909
Telephone: 1-800-786-5476
              303-786-8000
Fax: 303-939-9652

Appendix

Ways of Burning Joss Stick

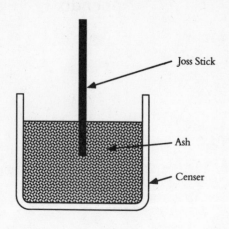

Joss Stick

Ash

Censer

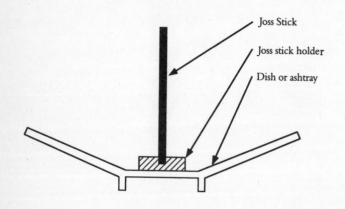

Joss Stick

Joss stick holder

Dish or ashtray

Using Incense to Scent a Room

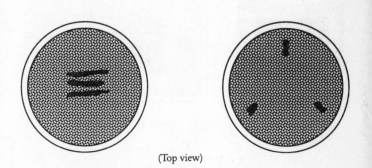

(Top view)

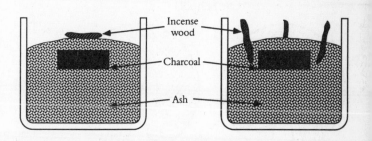

Incense wood

Charcoal

Ash

(Side view)

125

Shino Incense Censer

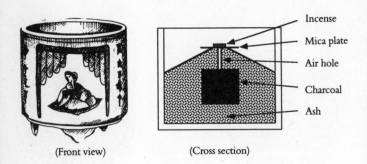

(Front view)   (Cross section)

Incense
Mica plate
Air hole
Charcoal
Ash

Incense Censer Ash Patterns (Top View)
(Oie School)

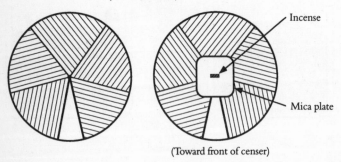

Incense

Mica plate

(Toward front of censer)

Utensils for the Incense Ceremony

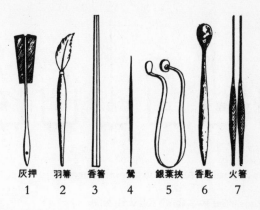

灰押	羽箒	香箸	鴬	銀葉挾	香匙	火箸
1	2	3	4	5	6	7

1. Ash press

2. Feather broom (to brush off the ashes on the lip of a censer)

3. Incense chopsticks (to handle small incense pieces)

4. Answer sheet holder

5. Silver tweezer (to handle mica plates)

6. Incense spoon (to place a small incense wood chip on a mica plate)

7. Metal chopsticks (to handle small pieces of charcoal and ashes)

Substitution ideas:
1. The end of a butter knife or the flat handle of a spoon. 2. A feather or piece of tissue paper. 3. A pair of tweezers. 4. A piece of paper. 5. A pair of tweezers. 6. A pair of tweezers. 7. Metal skewers.

How to Prepare a Censer

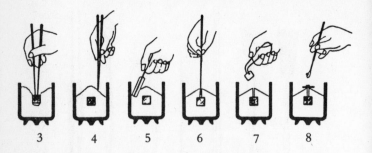

3   4   5   6   7   8

Have ready small incense wood chips for listening.

1. Fill the censer two-thirds full with ashes.

2. Heat a piece of charcoal (specifically suited for Koh-do) well till it becomes grayish white (you can do this over the kitchen range), and place this on the ashes in the censer.

3. Press the charcoal halfway down with metal chopsticks.

4. Quickly and lightly cover the charcoal with ashes, making a cone shape in the censer.

5. Quickly and gently press the ashes, making a neatly shaped mount.

6. With a metal chopstick, make an air hole reaching the charcoal, so that there is oxygen to keep it burning.

7. Place a mica plate on top of the mount (covering the air hole) using the tweezer, and press the center gently so that it will sit flat.

8. Now place a tiny chip of incense wood (a millimeter thin and half the length of a long grain rice) on the mica plate.

9. Place the censer flat on the palm of your left hand, and hold it securely by hooking your thumb on the lip of the censer. With your right hand, cover the censer, leaving a small opening between your thumb and index finger from which to inhale the incense fragrance.

Be sure to hold the censer flat. Do not tilt it. Do not inhale or exhale into the censer, or you will have a mess!

Traditional Room Layout and Seating Arrangement for the Incense Ceremony

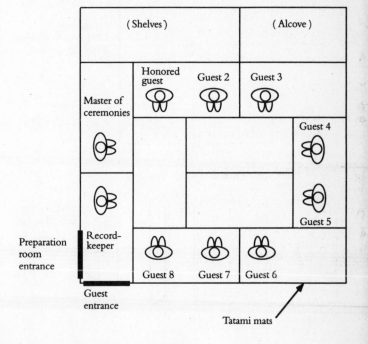

Tatami mats

Wrapping Incense for Kumikoh

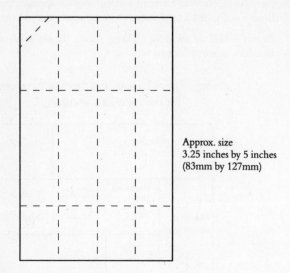

Approx. size
3.25 inches by 5 inches
(83mm by 127mm)

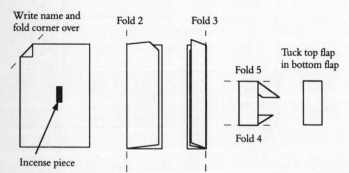

Write name and
fold corner over

Incense piece

Fold 2

Fold 3

Fold 5

Fold 4

Tuck top flap
in bottom flap

Participant's Answer Sheet for Kumikoh

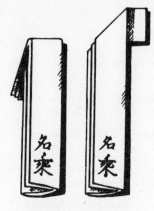

Participant's name

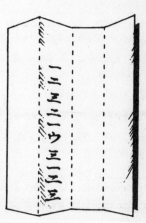

Participant's answers
(Example : 1, 2, 3, 2, 1, unknown . . .)

Further Reading

Ackerman, Diane. *A Natural History of the Senses*. New York: Random House, 1990.

Aston, W.G., II, trans. *Nihongi: Chronicles of Japan from the Earliest Times to A.D. 697*. Tokyo: Tuttle, 1971.

Boyer, Martha. *Catalogue of Japanese Lacquers*. Baltimore: Walters Art Gallery, 1970.

Corbin, Alain. *The Foul and the Fragrant: Odor and the French Social Imagination*. Cambridge, Mass.: Harvard University Press, 1986.

Gatten, Aileen. "A Wisp of Smoke." *Monumenta Nipponica* 32 (1977):35–48.

Hearn, Lafcadio. *In Ghostly Japan*. Rutland, Vt.: Tuttle, 1971.

Huizinga, Johan. *Homo Ludens*. Boston: Beacon Press, 1955.

Morris, Ivan. *The World of the Shining Prince*. New York: Penguin Books, 1979.

——————, trans. and ed. *The Pillow Book of Sei Shonagon*. Harmondsworth, Middlesex: Penguin Books, 1970.

Murasaki Shikibu. *The Tale of Genji*. Translated by Arthur Waley. Rutland, Vt.: Tuttle, 1972.

Watson, William, ed. *The Great Japan Exhibition: Art of the Edo Period 1600–1868*. London: Royal Academy of Arts, 1981.

Bibliography

Aston, W.G., II, trans. *Nihongi: Chronicles of Japan from the Earliest Times to A.D. 697.* Tokyo: Tuttle, 1973.

Corbin, Alain. *The Foul and the Fragrant: Odor and the French Social Imagination.* Cambridge, Mass.: Harvard University Press, 1986.

Geinoshi Kenkyukai. *Cha, hana, ko* (Tea, flowers, incense). *Nihon no Koten Geino 5.* Tokyo: Heibonsha, 1970.

Hachiya Soyu. *Zukai. Kodo no saho to kumiko* (Illustrations: the manners of Koh-do and kumiko). Tokyo: Yuzankaku, 1978.

Hayakawa Jinzo. *Kodo* (The Way of Incense). Tokyo: Yakumo shoin, 1943.

――――――. "Iwayuru Genjikozu ni tsuite" (About the so-called Genjikozu). *Nihon Daigaku Rikogakubu Ippan Kyoyo Kyoshitsu iho* 8 (1967):36–41.

Hayashi Ryoichi. *Shiruku rodo to Shosoin* (The Silk Road and Shosoin). *Nihon no Bijutsu 6.* Tokyo: Heibonsha, 1966.

Hearn, Lafcadio. *In Ghostly Japan.* Rutland, Vt.: Tuttle, 1971.

Isshoku Rikyo. *Ko no sho* (Book of incense). Tokyo: Kisho Kankokai, 1976.

Jakuren. "Kunshu ruisho" (Selections from incense anthologies). In *Gunsho ruiju* XII (no. 358):518–554. Tokyo: Keizai Zasshisha, 1900.

Kitaoji Isamitsu. *Kodo e no shotai* (Invitation to the Way of Incense). Tokyo: Hobunkan, 1978.

"Kodo" (The Way of Incense). *Kyoto* 305 (October 1976):13-72.

Kodo Bunka Kenkyukai. *Ko to Kodo* (Incense and the Way of Incense). Tokyo: Yuzankaku, 1989.

Murai Yasuhiko. "Cha, hana, ko no keifu" (Genealogy of tea, flowers, and incense), In *Cha, hana, ko*, edited by Geinoshi Kenkyukai. *Nihon no Koten Geino 5*. Tokyo: Heibonsha, 1970.

Sanjonishi Kin'osa. *Kumiko no Kansho* (Appreciation of incense games). Tokyo: Risosha, 1971.

——————. *Kodo: Rekishi to Bungaku* (The Way of Incense: history and literature). Tokyo: Tankosha, 1977.

Seidensticker, Edward, trans. *The Tale of Genji*. New York: Random House, 1985.

Shoyeido Koho-shitsu. *Kaori no hon* (The book of fragrances). Tokyo: Kodansha, 1988.

Sugimoto Buntaro. *Kodo* (The Way of Incense). Tokyo: Yuzankaku, 1977.

"Kaori no bunka" (The culture of fragrance). In *Nagomi* (March 1990). Kyoto: Tankosha, 1990.

Wada Gun'ichi. "Ranjatai" (Ranjatai incense). In *Nihon rekishi* 335 (April 1976):40-43.

Yamada Kentaro. *Nihon Koryo shi* (History of Japanese spices). Tokyo: Domeisha, 1979.

——————. *Koryo: Nihon no Nioi* (Spices: Japanese aromas). Tokyo: Hosei University Press, 1980.

DISCOVER JAPAN Words, Customs, and Concepts

The Japan Culture Institute

Short, practical descriptions of the words, ideas and customs of Japan.

"The one book you must have if you're heading for Japan..."—*Essex Journal*

Volume 1
Paperback: 216 pages, 110 x 182 mm, b/w photos, ISBN 0-87011-835-8
Volume 2
Paperback: 224 pages, 110 x 182 mm, b/w photos, ISBN 0-87011-836-6

THE ANATOMY OF DEPENDENCE

Takeo Doi, MD. Translated by John Bester

The classic analysis of *amae*, the indulging, passive love which supports an individual within a group, and a key concept in Japanese psychology.

"Profound insights not only into the character of Japan but into the nuances of dependency relationships."—Ezra Vogel

Paperback: 184 pages, 110 x 182 mm, ISBN 0-87011-494-8

THE ANATOMY OF SELF The Individual Versus Society

Takeo Doi, MD. Translated by Mark A. Harbison

A fascinating exploration of the role of the individual in Japan, and Japanese concepts of self-awareness, communication, and relationships.

"An excellent book."—Frank A. Johnson, MD., U.C. San Francisco

Paperback: 176 pages, 110 x 182 mm, ISBN 0-87011-902-8

APPRECIATIONS OF JAPANESE CULTURE

Donald Keene

The dean of Japanese studies provides a classic introduction to the beauties and intricacies of Japanese literature, offering an essential companion to the study of Japanese prose and poetry of all eras.

Paperback: 350 pages, 110 x 182 mm, ISBN 4-7700-0956-9

ON FAMILIAR TERMS A Journey Across Cultures

Donald Keene

The intimate and engaging memoirs of the renowned scholar and translator who "discovered" modern Japanese literature.

Paperback: 306 pages, 142 x 213 mm, ISBN 1-56836-129-7

PUBLIC PEOPLE, PRIVATE PEOPLE
Portraits of Some Japanese

Donald Richie

The private recollections of long-time Japan resident Donald Richie capture the personalities of certain Japanese people—some famous, some unknown—with insight, humor, and elegance.
"His portraits are unforgettable."—Tom Wolfe

Paperback: 212 pages, 110 x 182 mm, ISBN 4-7700-2104-6
Previously published as:*Some Japanese Portraits*, and *Geisha, Gangster, Neighbor, Nun*

THE ESSENCE OF ZEN
Dharma Talks Given in Europe and America

Sekkei Harada

An informal introduction to the fundamentals of Buddhist thought and the principles of Zen practice from one of the foremost Zen masters in Japan, specifically tailored for audiences in Europe and the United States.

Hardcover: 200 pages, 128 x 188 mm, ISBN 4-7700-2199-2

THE BOOK OF TEA

Kakuzo Okakura
Foreword and Afterword by Soshitsu Sen XV, Grand Tea Master, Urasenke School of Tea

The seminal text on the meaning and practice of tea. Written 80 years ago, the book is less about tea than it is about the philosophical and aesthetic traditions basic to Japanese culture.

Paperback: 160 pages, 110 x 182 mm, 8 B/W photos, ISBN 4-7700-1542-9

THE TEA CEREMONY New Edition

Sen'o Tanaka
Foreword by Edwin O. Reischauer Preface by Yasushi Inoue

A comprehensive look at the sources and inspiration of an ancient discipline by one of Japan's contemporary tea masters. Sen'o Tanaka traces the practice from its earliest origins to the present day, and examines in detail the individuals who helped it evolve.

Hardcover: 224 pages, 189 x 257 mm, 50 color plates, 50 b/w photos, 50 line drawings; glossary; index, ISBN 4-7700-2125-9

THE JAPANESE THROUGH AMERICAN EYES

Sheila K. Johnson

Anthropologist Sheila Johnson looks into the images and stereotypes of Japanese produced by American popular culture. A revealing look at movies, war propaganda, cartoons, and best-selling novels.

Paperback: 208 pages, 110 x 182 mm, ISBN 4-7700-1450-3, Territories: Japan only

BLUEPRINT FOR A NEW JAPAN
The Rethinking of a Nation

Ichiro Ozawa   Introduction by Sen. Jay Rockefeller

Political pundit Ozawa outlines the steps Japan must take to become a "normal" nation in the post-Cold War world.
"Nobody trying to understand Japan can afford to ignore this book."
—The Economist

Hardcover: 208 pages, 152 x 226 mm, ISBN 4-7700-1871-1
Paperback: 208 pages, 110 x 182 mm, ISBN 4-7700-2041-4
Territories: PB Japan only

THE THIRD CENTURY

Joel Kotkin & Yoriko Kishimoto

As the U.S. enters its third century it faces serious competition from Asia, but, the authors argue, it can withstand the challenge by adopting a realistic and resilient attitude.

Paperback: 304 pages, 110 x 182 mm, ISBN 4-7700-1452-X, Territories: Japan only

BLINDSIDE
Why Japan is Still on Track to Overtake the U.S. by the Year 2000

Eamonn Fingleton

"A book of fundamental originality and importance...Those who read it now will be ahead of the game." —James Fallows
"A brilliant book full of fresh insights that explode carefully nurtured myths about Japan, as well as much conventional wisdom." —Clyde Prestowitz

Paperback: 410 pages, 128 x 188 mm, ISBN 4-7700-2146-1, Territories: Japan only

ABOUT FACE
How I Stumbled onto Japan's Social Revolution

Clayton Naff

This unique analysis based on the personal and professional experiences of an American journalist reveals the changes occurring in the Japanese home and in the working world.
"The best guide to the internal pressures on Japan to change." — Chalmers Johnson

Paperback: 352 pages, 140 x 210 mm, notes, index, ISBN 1-56836-131-9

STRAITJACKET SOCIETY
An Insider's Irreverent View of Bureaucratic Japan

Masao Miyamoto   Foreword by Juzo Itami

A well-placed insider, Dr. Miyamoto presents a valuable and frank critique of the "closed society" of the Japanese bureaucracy. "Miyamoto has lifted the veil on Japan's powerful but oblique bureaucracy."—*Los Angeles Times*

Hardcover: 200 pages, 152 x 226 mm, ISBN 4-7700-1848-7
Paperback: 200 pages, 113 x 182 mm, ISBN 4-7700-1995-5

EDUCATING ANDY
The Experience of a Foreign Family in
the Japanese Elementary School System

Anne & Andy Conduit

Both insightful and humorous, this insider's view of the Japanese school system from the perspective of a blond, blue-eyed, twelve-year-old paints a revealing portrait of the Japanese character.

Paperback: 224 pages, 110 x 182 mm, b/w photos, ISBN 4-7700-1921-1

JAPAN FOR STARTERS
52 Things You Need to Know About Japan

Charles Danziger

Fifty-two sketches introduce the fundamentals of Japan's modern, traditional, and business worlds. Combining a hard-earned insider's knowledge with an irrepressible sense of fun, *Japan for Starters* is insightful, informative, and humorous—a delight to read.

Paperback: 174 pages, 110 x 182 mm, line drawings, ISBN 4-7700-2087-2
Previously published as *The American Who Couldn't Say Noh*.

WOMANSWORD
What Japanese Words Say About Women

Kittredge Cherry

Valuable insights into women's roles in Japan, their relations with men, and their view of themselves. An informal glossary with brief essays that collectively describe Japanese womanhood.

Paperback: 160 pages, 110 x 182 mm, ISBN 4-7700-1655-7

WORDS IN CONTEXT

Takao Suzuki   Translated by Akira Miura

One of Japan's foremost linguists offers a provocative analysis of the complex relationship between language and culture, psychology and lifestyle.

Paperback: 180 pages, 110 x 182 mm, 14 line illustrations, ISBN 0-87011-642-8

MANGA! MANGA! The World of Japanese Comics

Frederick L. Schodt   Introduction by Osamu Tezuka

Profusely illustrated with the most representative examples of the genre, this is the first book in English to explore the world of Japanese comics.

Paperback: 260 pages, 182 x 257 mm, 8 color pages, 185 b/w photos,
96 pages of comics stories, ISBN 0-87011-752-1

A FAR VALLEY   Four Years in a Japanese Village

Brian Moeran

An intimate portrayal of the rhythms of life in a rural community in a remote valley in southern Japan, masterfully captured through the joyful and tragic experiences of anthropologist Moeran and his family. "An honest and personal odyssey."—Alan Booth, author of *Looking for the Lost*
"This is the very best kind of book"—Richard Bowring, Cambridge University

Paperback: 264 pages, 140 x 210 mm, ISBN 4-7700-2301-4
Previously published as *Okubo Diary*.

NEIGHBORHOOD TOKYO

Theodore C. Bestor

This highly readable anthropological study of a small, urban neighborhood provides insights into the whole social structure of modern Japan.

Paperback: 368 pages, 110 x 182 mm, ISBN 4-7700-1496-1, Territories: Japan only

---

THE HIDDEN ORDER
Tokyo Through the Twentieth Century

Yoshinobu Ashihara   Translated by Lynne E. Riggs

Using architecture as a metaphor for culture, renowned Japanese architect Yoshinobu Ashihara offers an insider's look at the apparent chaos of Tokyo.

Hardcover: 160 pages, 150 x 220 mm, 100 b/w photos and illustrations,
ISBN 0-87011-912-5,
Paperback: 160 pages, 110 x 182 mm, 100 b/w photos and illustrations,
ISBN 4-7700-1664-6

THE COMPACT CULTURE
The Japanese Tradition of "Smaller is Better"

O-Young Lee   Translated by Robert N. Huey

A provocative study of Japan's tendency to make the most out of miniaturization—a study of a philosophy of living that reveals the essence of Japanese character.

Paperback: 196 pages, 110 x 182 mm, 23 b/w illustrations, ISBN 4-7700-1643-3

EXPOSURE Victims of Radiation Speak Out

The Chugoku Newspaper
Introduction by Robert J. Lifton   Translated by Kirsten McIvor

An award-winning investigation by a Hiroshima newspaper into nuclear pollution around the world, and the human costs of "peace-time" usage of nuclear energy.

Hardcover: 328 pages, 152 x 226 mm, 22 b/w photos, ISBN 4-7700-1623-9
Paperback: 328 pages, 110 x 182 mm, 22 b/w photos, ISBN 4-7700-2065-1

A CALL FOR PEACE
The Implications of Japan's War-Renouncing Constitution

Charles M. Overby

In this bilingual edition, long-time advocate for peace and resource conservation Charles Overby offers the war-and-violence-renouncing principles in Article 9 of the Japanese constitution as a basis for world peace.

Hardcover: 220 pages, 140 x 210 mm, ISBN 4-7700-2062-7

EACH ONE A HERO The Philosophy of Symbiosis

Kisho Kurokawa

Intercultural thoughts on the future of relations between cultures, nations, and peoples by a renowned architect and social critic.

Hardcover: 544 pages, 152 x 226 mm, ISBN 4-7700-2140-2

THE PACIFIC CENTURY
America and Asia in a Changing World

Frank Gibney

Traces the past one hundred and fifty years of the Pacific Basin region, from colonialism to nationalism, from military clashes to economic ones, and the outlook for the future. Companion to the PBS TV series.

Paperback: 608 pages, 148 x 210 mm, 130 b/w photos, index, ISBN 4-7700-1862-2
Territories: Japan only

THE END OF THE CENTURY The Future in the Past

Edited by Nobutoshi Hagihara, Akira Irie, George Nivat, & Philip Windsor

Thirty-one distinguished scholars from Europe, Russia, the U.S., and Japan gather to discuss and comment on themes ranging from the collapse of communism to the displacement of populations, the environment, and human rights.

Hardcover: 480 pages, 145 x 226 mm, index, ISBN 4-7700-2021-X

Abe, Kobo	**THE FACE OF ANOTHER** **THE RUINED MAP** **SECRET RENDEZVOUS**
Agawa, Hiroyuki	**CITADEL IN SPRING** **THE RELUCTANT ADMIRAL**
Ariyoshi, Sawako	**THE DOCTOR'S WIFE** **KABUKI DANCER** **THE RIVER KI**
Boehm, Deborah	**A ZEN ROMANCE**
Booth, Alan	**LOOKING FOR THE LOST** **THE ROADS TO SATA**
Dazai, Osamu	**BLUE BAMBOO** **SELF PORTRAITS**
Enchi, Fumiko	**THE WAITING YEARS**
Endo, Shusaku	**THE SAMURAI** **SILENCE**
Hamill, Pete	**TOKYO SKETCHES**
Ibuse, Masuji	**BLACK RAIN** **CASTAWAYS** **SALAMANDER** **WAVES**
Ikenami, Shotaro	**THE MASTER ASSASSIN** **BRIDGE OF DARKNESS**
Ikezawa, Natsuki	**STILL LIVES**
Inoue, Yasushi	**LOU-LAN** **TUN-HUANG**
Ishikawa, Yoshimi	**STRAWBERRY ROAD**
Kaiko, Takeshi	**INTO A BLACK SUN**
Kawabata, Yasunari	**HOUSE OF THE SLEEPING BEAUTIES** **THE LAKE** **THE TALE OF THE BAMBOO CUTTER**
Kita, Morio	**GHOSTS**
Kizaki, Satoko	**THE PHOENIX TREE** **THE SUNKEN TEMPLE**
Komatsu, Sakyo	**JAPAN SINKS**
Kuroyanagi, Tetsuko	**TOTTO-CHAN**
Maruya, Saiichi	**A MATURE WOMAN** **RAIN IN THE WIND** **SINGULAR REBELLION**
Matsumoto, Seicho	**POINTS AND LINES** **THE VOICE**

Mishima, Yukio	ACTS OF WORSHIP SUN AND STEEL
Miyazawa, Kenji	ONCE AND FOREVER
Miyabe, Miyuki	ALL SHE WAS WORTH
Murakami, Haruki	A WILD SHEEP CHASE HARD-BOILED WONDERLAND AND THE END OF THE WORLD DANCE DANCE DANCE
Murakami, Ryu	69 ALMOST TRANSPARENT BLUE COIN LOCKER BABIES
Nagai, Takashi	THE BELLS OF NAGASAKI
Nakagami, Kenji	SNAKELUST
Natsume, Soseki	BOTCHAN
Oda, Makoto	H: A HIROSHIMA NOVEL
Oe, Kenzaburo	JAPAN, THE AMBIGUOUS, AND MYSELF AN ECHO OF HEAVEN THE SILENT CRY THE CATCH NIP THE BUDS SHOOT THE KIDS A HEALING FAMILY
Sato, Masayoshi	SHOGUN'S GOLD
Setouchi, Harumi	THE END OF SUMMER
Shiga, Naoya	A DARK NIGHT'S PASSING
Shiina, Makoto	MY BOY
Shimada, Masahiko	DREAM MESSENGER
Tanizaki, Jun'ichiro	A CAT, A MAN, AND TWO WOMEN CHILDHOOD YEARS
Tasker, Peter	SILENT THUNDER
Tawada, Yoko	THE BRIDEGROOM WAS A DOG
Tsuji, Kunio	THE SIGNORE
Tsujii, Takashi	A SPRING LIKE ANY OTHER
Tsushima, Yuko	CHILD OF FORTUNE
Yamada, Amy	TRASH
Yamamoto, Michiko	BETTY-SAN
Yamasaki, Toyoko	THE BARREN ZONE
Yoshiyuki, Junnosuke	THE DARK ROOM
Yoshikawa, Eiji	FRAGMENTS OF A PAST MUSASHI TAIKO

153 E. 69th St.   212 988-6161

ANTHOLOGIES

A HISTORY OF JAPANESE LITERATURE
VOLUME 1: THE FIRST THOUSAND YEARS
VOLUME 2: THE YEARS OF ISOLATION
VOLUME 3: THE MODERN YEARS
A HISTORY OF JAPANESE LITERATURE: SET

MONKEY BRAIN SUSHI
New Tastes in Japanese Fiction

THE SHOWA ANTHOLOGY
Modern Japanese Short Stories

THE MOTHER OF DREAMS AND OTHER STORIES
Portrayals of Women in Modern Japanese Fiction

CRITICISM

THREE MODERN NOVELISTS
Soseki, Tanizaki, Kawabata

WANDERING GHOST
The Odyssey of Lafcadio Hearn

A READER'S GUIDE TO JAPANESE LITERATURE
New Edition

HAIKU

THE NARROW ROAD TO OKU

A HAIKU JOURNEY
Basho's The Narrow Road to a Far Province

MATSUO BASHO

AUTUMN WIND
A Selection from the Poems of Issa

THE HAIKU HANDBOOK
How to Write, Share, and Teach Haiku

THE HAIKU SEASONS
Poetry of the Natural World

HAIKU WORLD
An International Poetry Almanac